Cowgirl Prayers
A 365 Day Book of Prayers
Copyright © 2022 United States Copyright Office

All rights reserved. No part of this publication may be reproduced, stored in a retrieval system, or trans- mitted in any form or by any neans-electronic, mechanical, digital, photocopy, recording, or any other- except for brief quotations in printed reviews, without the prior permission of the publisher.

Cowgirl Prayers

A 365 Day Book of Prayers

Written by:
Katie Marie Chism

Contributions by:
Carly Elford
Courtney DeArcos

Editing Team:
Diane Lazear
Stan Jaowiak
Morgan Hanson
Mikaela Morris
Kiera Walker
Kandis Bowman

A Message from the Author

I am neither a writer nor a blogger. I am simply a cowgirl following a calling I felt from the Lord. Starting the Facebook page, *Cowgirl Prayers*, was a step outside my comfort zone, but God led the way. This book was also part of that calling, an even bigger step outside my comfort zone. Again, God led the way, and I am simply following that calling.

My prayer for this book is that just as the prayers spoke to those who followed the *Cowgirl Prayers* page, they will speak to readers of this book. The prayers are a collection of 365 days of prayers I posted on Facebook over a year and a half period.

You can read this book in a variety of ways. You can start right at Day 1 on January 1st, a perfect option for those getting the book for Christmas. You also can match your start date to the date on the prayer. For those days when you want a prayer in a specific area, the book has a theme index to collections of prayers.

Day 1
January 1st

Peace & Joy

Lord, tonight we pray for the cowgirl who needs to find her joy again. Somewhere between the rough patches, hard lessons learned, and daily headaches she's having a tough time finding joy in the journey. So, we pray Lord You give her direction and guide her heart to greater joys and a deeper relationship with You. We pray she steps away from the things that no longer serve You and shine Your light. We pray she sees the joy she brings others and be reminded of her purpose. May that purpose and passion in her heart remind her of the joy to be found in her journey. May she seek calm with You, and we pray You bring her hope and peace.

John 15:11
"I have told you these things so that My joy may be in you and your joy may be complete."

Amen

Day 2
January 2nd

Soft Place to Land

Lord, tonight we pray for the cowgirl that is struggling. Struggling to move on, struggling to keep up, struggling to find balance, or just struggling to keep her head above water. She may feel lost and not sure what turn to take next. Maybe she is tired of wrong turns and disappointments. Or maybe she is just tired of treading water trying to find a soft place to land. Whatever her situation, Lord, we pray she knows You see her, and You are with her. We pray even in her toughest hours she feels You nearby. We pray when she seeks You, You guide her. We pray when she falls, You restore her. And we pray that she knows in every step she is chosen and loved by You.

Romans 8:18
"I consider that our present sufferings are not worth comparing with the glory that will be revealed in us."

Amen

Day 3
January 3rd

The Horse that Made Us

Lord, tonight we pray thanks for the horses that have saved us, the ones that have made us, and the ones that have made us dream again. We pray thanks for the babysitters, the "old-faithfuls", and the retired champions in the pasture. These horses have built us, carried us through the highs and lows, and kept all our secrets. They have taught us patience, resilience, and lessons we didn't know we needed to learn. We pray thanks for the gift they are and the gifts they have given us. We are grateful for the blessing they are and the connection we have to You Lord, through them.

Proverbs 21:31
"The horse is made ready for the day of battle, but the victory belongs to the Lord."

Amen

Day 4
January 4th

Too Much

Lord, tonight we pray for the cowgirl that feels overwhelmed. She may be a little scared, stressed, anxious, angry, or a little bit of all of those things together. Her feelings are all over the place and she isn't sure which side is up. Your blessings abound around her and yet she can't seem to shake this funk she is in. Her heart hurts and the situation around her just feels like too much. She may have opened up to talk about it, or maybe she's kept it all inside. Whatever the situation Lord, we pray she knows You have never left her side. That in every emotion, You are there with her. We pray she seek You to calm her fears and anxiety. May she feel Your peace and comfort wash over her. Give her grace and mercy when she needs it, Lord. Fill her heart with Your love and remind her that no matter what she faces the battle has already been won.

Philippians 4:6-7
"Do not be anxious about anything, but in everything, by prayer and petition, with thanksgiving, present your requests to God. And the peace of God, which transcends all understanding, will guard your hearts and your minds in Christ Jesus."

Amen

Day 5
January 5th

Growth in Grace

Lord, tonight we pray for our cowgirl seeking growth. It may be growth in her career, her riding, or competitions. The thing about growth is that it tends to be uncomfortable, Lord. So, we pray she seeks Your guidance in the uncomfortable moments. For in these moments, she is finding the opportunity to make changes and seek new opportunities she wouldn't find in her comfort zone. We pray You provide these opportunities for growth, and we pray she takes the chance to make the change.

2 Peter 3:18
"But grow in grace, and in the knowledge of our Lord and Savior Jesus Christ. To Him be glory both now and forever."

Amen

Day 6
January 6th

Big Dreams

Lord, tonight we come to You to pray for the cowgirl with big dreams...dreams and goals that others may laugh at or turn up their nose at. But it doesn't matter if she's 15 or 50. If You have put them in her heart, You will guide her on that journey. For the passion You have put in her heart will lead to Your purpose for her. So tonight, Lord, we pray she doesn't get discouraged by what others say or do. We pray she seek You and strengthen that relationship with You so that You may continue to guide her through her journey of big dreams.

John 15:5
"I am the vine; you are the branches. Whoever abides in Me and I in him, he it is that bears much fruit, for apart from Me you can do nothing."

Amen

Day 7
January 7th

Renew Faith

Lord, tonight we pray for our cowgirl that needs to renew her faith. She holds You in her heart Lord, but she has felt the trials of this world weigh it down. She longs to feel Your peace, Lord-the peace that passes all understanding that only You can provide. She's thankful for Your grace when she knows she fails You, and she prays for Your forgiveness when she lets it all get the best of her. So, we pray big love over her, Your unconditional love. May it sweep over her and warm her soul. May Your peace lift up her faith and take the weight off her heart.

2 Corinthians 4:16
"Therefore we do not lose heart. Though outwardly we are wasting away, yet inwardly we are being renewed day by day."

Amen

Day 8
January 8th

Faith in Fear

Dear Lord, tonight we pray for the cowgirl who is afraid. Afraid of a big change, afraid of a closing door, afraid of a new beginning. She runs to You for answers but still feels a little unsure. Quiet her mind and ease her fears. Give her the confidence to let go, the confidence to step up, or simply to remain still and wait for Your clear direction. No matter what she is facing, remind her...

Isaiah 41:10
"So do not fear, for I am with you; do not be dismayed, for I am your God. I will strengthen you and help you; I will uphold you with my righteous right hand."

Amen

Day 9
January 9th

Hope & Healing

Lord, tonight we pray for the cowgirl waiting for answers. Although she knows You hold all the answers in the palm of Your hand, it is still hard to wait for Your timing, Lord. She may be waiting for results from the doctor, a job interview, or loan application for a new home. She prays for Your guidance over the answers she seeks. May she look to You when her mind gets anxious. We pray You calm her heart and her mind, be with her in her waiting and comfort her if the answer is one that is hard to swallow. We pray she thanks You in all things.

Psalm 33:20-22
"We wait in hope for the Lord; He is our help and our shield. In Him our hearts rejoice, for we trust in His holy name."

Amen

Day 10
January 10th

Seeking Purpose

Lord, tonight we pray for the cowgirl seeking her purpose. She prays to see the opportunity You intend for her to use the talents and gifts You have given her. She prays to be a light for You, a place for others to look and see You. Her testimony of her journey to You and with You is a gift she wishes to share with others. We pray Lord, You give her the opportunity. Sometimes she wonders if the path she is on is the right path or if she has strayed with her own desires. May You guide her and make her paths straight. May she seek You and find her answers.

Romans 8:28
"And we know that in all things God works for the good of those who love him, who have been called according to his purpose."

Amen

Day 11th
January 11th

Peace & Perseverance

Lord, tonight we pray for the cowgirl facing a challenge. She feels the pressure, she sees the mountain that needs to be moved. She knows she must be strong and steadfast to see this through. So, she prays for Your strength and guidance, Lord. She prays for renewed faith and patience to persevere. May You be with her, guide her, and strengthen her every step of the way.

James 1:12
"Blessed is the one who perseveres under trial because, having stood the test, that person will receive the crown of life that the Lord has promised to those who love Him."

Amen

Day 12th
January 12th

Reaffirmed Strength

Lord, tonight we pray for the cowgirl ready for new beginnings. It may be a new foal/calf this spring, or a new horse in training. Maybe it's a new job that allows more barn/home time, or maybe she just knows she needs a change, even if she isn't sure what it is yet. As exciting as new changes can be Lord, they can also be a little scary. So, we ask that You be with her as she steps out into faith, knowing You have her back. Her hope is in You Lord, may she soar like the eagles into her new beginning.

Isaiah 40:31
"Those who hope in the Lord will renew their strength. They will soar on wings like eagles; they will run and not grow weary; they will walk and not be faint."

Amen

Day 13th
January 13th

Finding Peace

Lord, tonight we pray for the cowgirl seeking peace. She's learning to find peace in Your plan even when it doesn't match her own. She's learning to find peace in the journey even in the hardest steps. And she's learning to find peace in the situations she never saw coming. Learning to find peace is a process that takes an open heart and an open mind. Because without them she will fail to see the opportunity to rest in Your peace, so we pray she finds both. We pray for grace and mercy along the journey in her quest for peace. May she seek Your guidance along the way.

John 16:33
"I have told you all this so that you may have peace in Me. Here on earth, you will have many trials and sorrows. But take heart because I have overcome the world."

Amen

Day 14
January 14th

Release Control

Lord, tonight we pray for the cowgirl that must give up control. Not that she ever really had it anyway, but perhaps the illusion of it. But this time everything feels completely out of her control in the most heart-wrenching way. Because she knows only You hold the answers, and only You can determine the outcome and how it effects the future ahead of her. So now more than ever she needs Your peace, she needs Your guidance and direction. She needs Your mercy and grace when her patience runs thin, and her anxiety takes over. Forgive her for wanting to have the answers sooner than You plan. Forgive her for wishing she could have control, even though in her heart she prays Your will be done, Lord. Comfort her when the tears roll down her cheeks in the uncertain hours. We pray Lord, that You fill her with Your unconditional love. May she pray the prayers with big faith to move mountains. And may she praise You in this storm.

Psalm 59:16
"But I will sing of Your strength, in the morning I will sing of Your love; for You are my fortress, my refuge in times of trouble."

Amen

Day 15
January 15th

Allow Grace

Lord, tonight we pray for the cowgirl that needs to give herself some grace. She is so giving of kind words and encouragement to others, but she fails to do the same for herself. We pray she remembers it's ok to hold herself to a high standard, but it's also ok to allow herself grace and room to breathe. We pray that she remembers the forgiveness and mercy that You provide Lord, each and every day. Even on the days she feels undeserving Lord, we pray You fill her with Your unconditional love. We pray that she learns to treat herself with the same kindness she extends to others. May she allow herself to receive Your grace and let it wash over her.

Hebrews 4:16
"So let us come boldly to the throne of our gracious God. There we will receive His mercy, and we will find grace to help us when we need it most."

Amen

Day 16
January 16th

Be A Light

Lord, tonight we pray for the cowgirl that needs some perspective. It's so easy sometimes to get caught up in where you want to be and what you need to do to get there, that you forget to enjoy the process. She has goals and plans with the passion You put in her heart Lord, but we pray she remembers Your purpose along the way. We pray she remembers; win or learn, the glory belongs to You. We pray she remembers You don't care what the results read, you care what she does with the opportunity. We pray she remembers to be a light, we pray she remembers every opportunity comes with a responsibility to shine for You. So, we pray thanks Lord, for every opportunity, may You guide her steps, and fill her heart.

Matthew 5:16
"Let Your light shine before others, that they may see Your good deeds and glorify Your Father in heaven."

Amen

Day 17
January 17th

Stay the Course

Tonight, Lord, we pray for the cowgirl that needs to persevere. The journey she is on, the race she is running has worn at her faith. The struggles, the dark valleys, and the hills she has climbed make the road a bit rough. And so somedays she wonders if she is on the right course. We pray Lord, that she remembers that no journey is meant to be smooth, but she is still called to find the joy in it. We pray she remembers that even in the darkest valley and the biggest hurdles, that You walk with her. May she remember that she was created for this journey, and You have equipped her with all the tools, she need only look to You for guidance.

Hebrews 12 1-2
"Let us run with endurance the race God has set before us. We must keep our eyes on Jesus, who leads us and makes our faith complete."

Amen

Day 18
January 18th

One Day At A Time

Lord, tonight we pray for the cowgirl that is taking it one day at a time. One day of healing, one day of a new job, a new relationship, one day of starting over. Her mind tries to race ahead and find worries. But she digs deep each day finding the faith to take it one step at a time. She knows only You know the future and You hold it and her in Your hands. We pray for peace Lord; we pray You bring comfort on the days it's hard to take those steps. We pray for Grace and Mercy when her mind tries to race ahead. We pray she feel your guidance no matter the path that lay ahead.

Psalm 37:23-24
"The LORD makes firm the steps of the one who delights in him; though he may stumble, he will not fall, for the LORD upholds him with his hand."

Amen

Day 19
January 19th

Moving Mountains

Lord, tonight we come to You for the Cowgirl that feels stuck. It may be in a tough job, the wrong relationship, or just in a rut with her horse. She knows this is just a valley Lord, but she's having a hard time seeing the other side. We ask You to remind her that You move mountains Lord, that nothing is impossible for You and it only takes a mustard seed of faith. Renew that faith in her Lord, to take that step, to be strong and courageous, and put one foot in front of the other... Forward! Just as the mountains, You are right beside her Lord, as she pushes onward. Just as the seasons change, so too will her situation Lord, but we pray You give her the strength to keep moving forward to get to the other side.

Mark 11:23
"Truly, I say to you, whoever says to this mountain, 'Be taken up and thrown into the sea,' and does not doubt in his heart, but believes that what he says will come to pass, it will be done for him."

Amen

Day 20
January 20th

Walk without Fear

Lord, tonight we pray for the cowgirl that needs to take a deep breath. She finds herself getting frustrated or worried about things that haven't even happened yet. Her anxiety gets the best of her somedays and she feels like she gets so distracted by future worries that she forgets to live in the here and now. We pray for her to take that deep breath and soak up all You have to offer. Fill her with the peace that You carry all her days, past, present, and future. Rest her anxious mind with the promise that she will never be alone with You in her heart. May she find comfort in You and Your promises to become like the Proverbs 31 woman.

Proverbs 31:25
"For She is clothed with strength and dignity, and she laughs without fear of the future."

Amen

Day 21
January 21st

Renewed Spirit

Lord, tonight we pray for the cowgirl that has had a tough day. Maybe a day of delays, disappointments or disaster. Or perhaps a little bit of all of them. She felt like everything she touched turned to trouble and she just prayed for the sun to set so she could find her pillow. We pray Lord, You meet her right where she is, whether it's fixing fence, fixing dinner or somewhere in between. We pray You restore her confidence in herself through You.

Lamentations 3:22-23
"Because of the LORD's great love we are not consumed, for His mercies never fail. They are new every morning; great is your faithfulness."

We pray Lord, as she lays her head on that pillow that she feels You refresh her soul and feel Your mercy cover her. May she wake in the morning with a renewed spirit ready to take on the world.

Amen

Day 22
January 22nd

Peace Along the Path

Lord, tonight we pray for the cowgirl seeking growth and change. It may be in her personal or professional life. Or maybe it's in her relationships, with others or with You. No matter the situation Lord, we know that it is not always an easy road to walk. Although we know it's worth the struggle, sometimes it can be intimidating. Sometimes it can be difficult to even know where to start. We pray Lord, for Your guidance and direction. We pray You bring her peace to know she is following the path You have for her. May she seek You with each step. Bring her mercy for the days that she walks astray, gently guide her back on course.

Psalm 24:4-5
"Show me the right path, O LORD; point out the road for me to follow. Guide me in Your truth and teach me, for You are God my Savior, and my hope is in You all day long."

Amen

Day 23
January 23rd

Good Enough?

Lord, tonight we pray for the cowgirl that feels like she isn't good enough. All that she tries or all she is working toward seems to fall short. She feels like she takes one step forward and two steps back. No matter what it seems she is working at or trying to be, nothing seems to add up to getting where she wants to be. Lord, first we pray You lift her up in Your truth. We pray she remembers that fear is a liar. That the lies she hears in her mind do not come from You. We pray she remembers to find joy in the journey and that not everything revolves around the destination. Sometimes our greatest joy and lessons can be found and learned along the way. May she see the steps she takes as steps in Faith, regardless of the direction. And if she is walking in Faith, she is walking with You.

2 Corinthians 3:5
"Not that we are sufficient in ourselves to claim anything as coming from us, but our sufficiency is from God"

Amen

Day 24
January 24th

Preparation with a Purpose

Tonight's prayer is for our cowgirl who is feeling anxious. For she feels the plans and dreams You have laid on her heart, but yet she struggles to see the path or understand the journey. She wants to work hard and give You the glory as it comes full circle, but she's having trouble seeing around the bend. We pray Lord, she remembers all good things come in YOUR timing, not hers. We pray she remembers You see the whole circle and know every piece of the puzzle. She need not run ahead to see what's next for You already have it planned. We pray she remembers You are preparing her for the journey ahead and to enjoy each step and each day because it is in preparation for those things You have placed in her heart. Without proper preparation she would not be ready for the things she seeks, so we pray she is patient to receive to Your full plan.

Isaiah 40:31
"But those who trust in the LORD will find new strength. They will soar high on wings like eagles. They will run and not grow weary. They will walk and not faint."

Amen

Day 25
January 25th

Seeking Comfort

Lord, tonight we pray for the cowgirl seeking comfort. Disappointments and heartbreak have worn her down. She puts on a brave face, puts her head down and buries herself in the work around her. But down inside her heart begs for a soft place to land. A place where she doesn't have to carry the weight of the world on her shoulders. She prays for a place to cry the tears she holds inside, and no one sees. A place where she just feels the love and peace that You provide, Lord. We pray that you meet her right where she is, Lord. Find her in her frustrations, heal her in her heartache, and meet her in her mistakes. Pull her from her darkness and show her light and love. Bring comfort to her heart and mercy to her soul. We ask this all because scripture tells us:

Psalm 34:17-18
"The LORD hears his people when they call to him for help. He rescues them from their troubles. The LORD is close to the brokenhearted and saves those who are crushed in spirit."

Amen

Day 26
January 26th

Friendship

Tonight, Lord, we pray for the cowgirl that is thankful for the friends that have turned into family. She is thankful for the ones that have showed up when no one else did. Thankful for the ones that she always knew were in her corner. And grateful the ones that believed in her when she didn't believe in herself. She prays thanks over the ones that were never more than a phone call away, whether it was for a colicky baby or horse, they were there. She may not have always had her own family there, but they were. We pray for blessings and protection over them, Lord.

Proverbs 27:9
"A sweet friendship refreshes the soul."

Amen

Day 27
January 27th

Pause, Breath, Focus

Dear Lord, tonight we pray for the cowgirl that just needs to breathe and draw closer to you. She may feel overwhelmed, impatient, exhausted, any combination of those things. Sometimes her days just rush past her in a blur and whirlwind of emotions, and she forgets what matters-a relationship with You. We pray she takes pause and remembers to put You first, Lord. Because she knows when her strength is in You, she will not fail. We pray she takes time to focus and pursue that relationship because we know it will only make her stronger. We pray as she takes that deep breath tonight, that You breathe life back into her and bring her peace.

Psalm 46:5
"God is within her, she will not fail; God will help her when morning comes."

Amen

Day 28
January 28th

Headed for Healing

Lord, tonight we pray for the cowgirl overcoming injury/illness. It may be her horse, or it may be her own. It feels like so long since they have felt like themselves Lord, and they wish the rough days would pass a little faster. Be with her Lord, as she puts one foot in front of the other and nurses back to health. If it's a mystery lameness Lord, we pray you bring the right vet to shed light on the problem. Let her remember the good days of riding or competing with ease and joy and give her peace to know those days will come again.

Jeremiah 30:17
"I will restore your health and heal your wounds", declares the LORD."

Amen

Day 29
January 29th

Making A Way

Lord, tonight we pray for the cowgirl feeling like she has run out of road. She has run out of answers. She feels like she has walked down a long alley and all the doors have shut. She needs Your guidance Lord, to push through this roadblock. She battles between the faith in her heart and the negativity in her mind. We pray Lord, that you lift her up from the darkness in her mind. Restore her faith and open the doors in her mind. We pray she takes a deep breath and lets You in and allows You to take control of her life. Guide her back to the path You have for her. Give her peace in her heart. May she feel her patience restored as she allows You to make a way where it seems there is no way.

Isaiah 43:16
"I am the LORD, who opened a way through the waters, making a dry path through the sea."

Amen

Day 30
January 30th

Holy Spirit Come

Lord, tonight we pray for the cowgirl that needs to be filled with Your spirit. She needs to be filled with Your strength, power, and love so that she may rise above and soar on wings like eagles. Right now, she feels empty. She has tried to fill the emptiness with things if this world and that has only left her feeling lonely, unworthy, and discouraged. We pray Lord, that she feels Your love surrounding her and filling her soul. May she breathe in new life and feel Your strength renewing her spirit. We pray her eyes are opened to Your love and her heart seeks Your guidance.

Galatians 5:22
"But the fruit of the Spirit is love, joy, peace, patience, kindness, goodness, faithfulness."

Amen

Day 31
January 31st

Reaffirmed Trust

Lord, tonight we pray for the cowgirl needing to trust. Trust Your plan, trust her heart, trust the guidance that You provide, Lord. She prays diligently and works hard day in and day out to pursue the passion You put in her heart, and yet she has somehow lost her confidence. This world has broken her heart and stolen the innocent trust she once had. We pray Lord that You restore her, we pray You lift up her heart and breathe life and love back into it. We pray she remembers that she can trust Your word, and that You won't fail her. May she lay her brokenness at Your feet and trust that You will return it to her whole again. Give her grace and mercy to forgive the hurt of her past and heal her to have faith to trust again.

Psalm 143:8
"Let the morning bring me word of Your unfailing love, for I have put my trust in You. Show me the way I should go, for to You I entrust my life."

Amen

Day 32
February 1st

Relationship Trouble

Lord, tonight we pray for the cowgirl in a struggling relationship. It may be a friendship, a strained family relationship, or a troubled marriage. Struggles such as these tend to feel all encompassing, never ending, and discouraging. Breakdowns in communication and lack of understanding dig deep into the hearts of those involved. So, we pray Lord, for Your intervention. We pray You shine Your light into the darkness and may Your truth cover the lies. We pray for Your mercy and grace to cover the hurt hearts.

Ephesians 4: 2-3
"Always be humble and gentle. Be patient with each other, making allowance for each other's faults because of your love. Make every effort to keep yourselves united in the Spirit, binding yourselves together with peace."

Amen

Day 33
February 2nd

Grasping goals

Tonight, Lord, we pray for the cowgirl whose dreams seem bigger than her pocketbook. She has a passion that You placed in her heart Lord, but sometimes it seems just beyond her grasp. She works hard day in and day out, long beyond a typical 9-5. Lord, give her comfort in knowing that You are working right beside her, helping lay the steps and foundation for her journey ahead. Her work and wait are not in vain, give her patience and courage to keep pushing onward towards those goals.

Philippians 4:19
"And my God will supply every need of yours according to his riches in glory in Christ Jesus."

Amen

Day 34
February 3rd

Break Free

Lord, tonight we come to You for the cowgirl who carries a burden she needs to let go. It may be a mistake she made in the past or a problem she couldn't fix. It's a hurt she tries to hide from the world afraid for others to see. She holds on to it thinking she deserves to hurt in order to pay for the wrong. But tonight, we want to remind her that the price has already been paid in full. The ultimate price You paid for us all so we could be forgiven. She need only to ask to be set free. Tonight, we pray that she come to You Lord, to hand over the hurt in exchange for peace and forgiveness in her heart.

Isaiah 10:27
"God will remove the burden from your shoulder and destroy the yoke on your neck."

Amen

Day 35
February 4th

Work Hard

Tonight, we pray for the cowgirl running on empty, Lord. From sunup to sundown and so many hours in between, she is on go. From livestock to kiddos she's chasing, feeding, or cleaning up after one or all of them. The work never ends and sometimes it's thankless. We pray that she knows in her heart that You see her and are grateful of her stewardship. Tonight, we ask You to fill her tank with praise for a job well done. Fill it with peace that only You can provide. And fill it with Joy that she is doing Your work and being a light for You in all she does.

Romans 12: 11-12
"Never be lazy but work hard and serve the Lord enthusiastically. Rejoice in hope, be patient in tribulation, be constant in prayer."

Amen

Day 36
February 5th

All the Things

Lord, tonight we pray for the cowgirl that is trying to be all the things. A wife, a mom, a sister, a daughter, a friend. A businesswoman, a horse woman, a home keeper. She wears a lot of hats, but sometimes they don't all fit, especially not all at once. Sometimes she feels like a jack of all trades, but master of none. Eventually something gives and it comes crashing down around her. So, we pray Lord, that You meet her right where she is whether it's 2 am in the barn with a fresh born foal, or 5 am making breakfast and bottles.

We pray You breathe life back into her heart and reignite the fire that fuels her passion behind it all. We pray You remind her that even when she doesn't feel like it, You have equipped her to be all she is called to be and that she is worthy of praise for the work she endures. May she find peace in the hustle, and joy in the journey. And when it all gets to be too much Lord, we pray she lays it at Your feet knowing You will always pick it up for her.

Matthew 11: 28-29
"Then Jesus said, 'Come to me, all of you who are weary and carry heavy burdens, and I will give you rest. Take My yoke upon you. Let Me teach you, because I am humble and gentle at heart, and you will find rest for your souls.'"

Amen

Day 37
February 6th

Changes

Dear Lord, tonight we come to You to pray for the cowgirl seeking change. It may be a change she wants, one she needs, or one she hopes for, but fears. Change can be exciting, but it can also bring anxiety of the unknown. Some changes come easier than others, and some she spends every day working towards. As she sets her sights towards the change Lord, we pray she seek Your guidance and direction. May the changes be in accordance with Your will. Give her grace and mercy on the days she feels unworthy of the change. Bring her peace on the days that overwhelm her. Remind her that her strength is in You, and through You all things are possible.

Isaiah 43:18-19
"Forget the former things; do not dwell on the past. See, I am doing a new thing! Now it springs up; do you not perceive it? I am making a way in the wilderness and streams in the desert."

Amen

Day 38
February 7th

Under Pressure

Lord, tonight we pray for the cowgirl that is feeling pressure. Pressure to be better, faster, prettier, more- always something more. She looks around her and feels like those around her have it all together, all the answers that she doesn't have. The pressure sets in, the pressure to find the answers so she can finally be more. And so, we pray Lord that You remind her that she is perfectly and wonderfully made. Remind her that she is equipped to do and be all that You have created her to be. We pray You surround her with the strength to look past the highlight reel of other's lives. May she look in the mirror and see the beauty that You created in her. We pray she seeks You when she feels the pressure build, may she lay those worries at Your feet to be washed away by You.

Ephesians 2:10
"For we are God's masterpiece, created in Christ Jesus to do good works, which God prepared in advance for us to do"

Amen

Day 39
February 8th

Devine Intervention

Lord, tonight we pray for the cowgirl that needs You to move. She prays desperately to see Your hand lay over her life. She needs a change in her circumstances. We pray for You to remove the fear, the pain, the desperation. Replace it with Your healing, strength, grace, and peace. She is praying for Your intervention to make the change she can see. In Jesus' name, we pray for You to move in her life and be the change that she needs.

Deuteronomy 20:4
"For the LORD your God is the one who goes with you to fight for you against your enemies to give you victory."

Amen

Day 40
February 9th

Calling out

Tonight, Lord, we pray for the cowgirl looking for answers. Needing answers for the questions in her heart. Whether it's for a decision she needs to make or to solve a problem, we pray she turns to You for all she seeks. Not only do You have the answers Lord, but You also carry the relief for the anxiety that the questions carry. As cowgirls, our days are filled with many things to be solved, but sometimes we are left still needing answers for things. So, we pray she turns to You when those answers are a little harder to find.

Psalm 91:15
"He will call upon me, and I will answer Him; I will be with Him in trouble, I will deliver Him and honor Him."

Amen

Day 41
February 10th

Dig Deep

Lord, tonight we pray for the cowgirl that needs to dig deep. She needs to dig deep into her faith and find courage. She needs to dig deep into her prayer life and find strength. She needs to dig deep into her passion and find her purpose. On the surface she is content with the day to day, but when she looks deeper, she sees so much more. So much more that she is capable of and longs for. We pray Lord, that whatever drives her, whatever passion You have put in her heart that You guide her to that deeper level. Give her strength and courage to push through the struggles. Give her resilience to dig deeper beyond what is average or easy. May she draw closer to You every step of the way as You guide her to becoming all You have planned for her to be.

Ephesians 2:10
"For we are God's masterpiece. He has created us anew in Christ Jesus, so we can do the good things He planned for us long ago."

Amen

Day 42
February 11th

Slow Down

Tonight, we pray for the cowgirl that needs a little slow down. With so much on her plate, her days sometimes just feel like a blur. She wants to enjoy the moments, but sometimes she gets too caught up in the "what's next" and misses the moments. She's grateful for all the opportunities all around her, but sometimes she feels like she misses out on the blessings right in front of her. We pray Lord, for strength to find pause in her days and find joy in the journey. We pray she lays any burdens and distractions at Your feet. Give her rest and take her burdens so she can find peace.

Psalm 55:22
"Cast your burden on the LORD, and he will sustain you."

Amen

Day 43
February 12th

Your Will Be Done

Lord, tonight we pray for the cowgirl that prays for Your will to be done. All her plans, her stress, her worries, her wants, her desires Lord, she lays them at Your feet. She prays for her will to align with Yours. She seeks what You want for her and prays to walk the steps You have for her. She knows no matter the scenario that Your will is greater and better than hers. Although her mind may try to override, she prays for Your guidance to persevere in her soul. She prays to be Your hands and feet, bring Your words to her lips, and may she shine Your light.

Psalm 143:10
"Teach me to do Your will, for You are my God. May Your gracious Spirit lead me forward on a solid ground"

Amen

Day 44th
February 13th

Give it to God

Lord, tonight we pray for the cowgirl that lays it all at Your feet. The job, the relationship, her finances, her health, and her circumstances. Whatever she is holding Lord, she is setting it down. Her shoulders and mind have grown heavy, and she finally realizes she wasn't meant to carry it alone. Many have told her You won't give her more than she can handle, but the truth is it is more than she can handle. It's more than she can handle alone, and she was never meant to. We pray for her heart Lord, as she finally releases the hurt she has held inside. We pray You flood her soul with your peace as she lays it down. Cover her in mercy and grace as she steps out into a new day without the weight of the world on her shoulders. We pray her eyes are opened to the relief and transition of turning it over to You.

Psalm 55:22
"Cast your burden upon the LORD and He will sustain you; He will never let the righteous be shaken."

Amen

Day 45
February 14th

Find Power in Purpose

Lord, tonight we pray for the cowgirl that doesn't feel comfortable. It may be in her work, a relationship, or in her own skin. Maybe she doesn't feel safe to be herself for fear of judgement. Or maybe she doesn't feel like she lives up to the comparison of others around her. We pray for You to wrap her in Your unconditional love. We pray that no matter the conditions this world may put on "acceptance", that Your love is freely given. We pray that she remembers she is carefully and wonderfully made, and that she was created in Your image. We pray she find strength to walk away from things or people that do not empower her and see the gifts she has to offer. We pray that not only she would see Your grace pour over her, but may Your light shine bright through her.

1 Corinthians 15:10
"But by the grace of God I am what I am, and His grace toward me was not in vain. On the contrary, I worked harder than any of them, though it was not I, but the grace of God that is with me."

Amen

Day 46
February 15th

A Light in our Darkness

Lord, tonight we pray for the cowgirl that feels alone. She may feel alone in a new situation, or maybe she feels like no one else understands how she feels. She may feel alone even when she's in a crowded room. Being alone is sometimes a welcome feeling as a cowgirl she is used to getting things done by herself. But sometimes the loneliness starts to creep in as she wishes she had someone else to share in the highs and lows. We pray Lord, for those around her to take notice and lift her up. May friends and family find the time to reach out to her. And we pray Lord, that she remembers that with You in her heart she is never alone, and that You are always there to listen. We pray You bring her comfort and may she always feel You near.

Micah 7:8
"When I fall, I shall rise; when I sit in darkness, the LORD will be a light to me."

Amen

Day 47
February 16th

Put away the Past

Lord, tonight we pray for the cowgirl that is trying to outrun her past. She has worked hard to turn herself around and walk away from the life she left behind. She knows You have forgiven her Lord, but sometimes she struggles to forgive herself. We pray Lord, that she remembers that You already paid the ultimate price to give forgiveness to all. We pray that You cover her in your unconditional love and grace. May she feel Your love cover her and bring her peace for she no longer must live in her past. It has been wiped clean and made new. We pray she finds strength and renewed faith in realizing Your forgiveness is enough.

2 Corinthians 5:17
"This means that anyone who belongs to Christ has become a new person. The old life is gone; a new life has begun!"

Amen

Day 48
February 17th

New Day, New Opportunity

Lord, tonight we pray for the cowgirl that is ready for a new day. She needs a new dawn to shed new light. She prays for new opportunity and fresh faith with the morning light. The days have been long and so have the nights. We pray You give her strength as she moves forward. Bring her rest tonight and restore her weary mind. Give her fresh perspective and give her peace as You take control and carry her burden.

Lamentations 3: 22-23
"Because of the Lord's great love we are not consumed, for his compassions never fail. They are new every morning; great is your faithfulness."

Amen

Day 49
February 18th

Empty Cup

Lord, tonight we pray for the cowgirl that is running out of steam. It may be a momma that is pouring from an empty cup. Maybe it's the cowgirl running on fumes, chasing dreams and white lines on the highway. Or maybe she is tired of burning the candle at both ends and still barely making ends meet. Whatever the situation Lord, we pray You meet her right where she is. At home, at work, on the road, in the field, or rocking a baby, remind her You are with her. Hold her and cover her in Your grace. Restore her and remind her that You are with her through every trial and every triumph. May she seek You and find Your guidance.

Psalm 119:105
"Your word is a lamp to guide my feet and a light for my path."

Amen

Day 50
February 19th

Adjust Focus

Lord, tonight we pray for our cowgirls that need to take a step back and adjust their focus. She has been working so hard with her head down that she has forgotten to look up and see the world around her. We pray she remembers to take the time to enjoy the journey, not just the grind. There is plenty of work to be done, but there is also plenty of joy to be found if only she takes a minute to look. We pray she takes the time to look to You and see the peace and joy You provide over all she does.

Romans 15:13
"I pray that God, the source of hope, will fill you completely with joy and peace because you trust in Him. Then you will overflow with confident hope through the power of the Holy Spirit."

Amen

Day 51
February 20th

Small Things

Lord, tonight we pray for the cowgirl struggling with the little things. It may be things with her career, her relationships, or herself. Sometimes she finds herself hanging up on the little things even though she knows there are much bigger worries at hand. She looks around her and knows that Your blessings surround her, but still finds herself frustrated at small inconveniences. So, we pray for balance, Lord. We pray You bring her grace through the rivers and valleys of life. May she find just as much JOY in the small things as she sometimes does frustration. We pray she remembers that You didn't call her to walk an easy path, You called her to be a light that shines for You always. We pray even in her darkest moments she looks to You and finds her light to shine.

James 1: 2-3
"Dear brothers and sisters, when troubles of any kind come your way, consider it an opportunity for great joy, for you know that when your faith is tested, your endurance has a chance to grow."

Amen

Day 52
February 21st

Step with the Spirit

Lord, tonight we pray for the cowgirl that is taking small steps with big faith. She has faith in Your promises Lord, and she knows You will be with her every step of the way. But big steps are too much right now, so she takes little ones each day in the right direction. She makes small moves to move big mountains because she knows with You she can do all things. We pray You bring her strength and comfort as she moves through this journey. We pray You give her courage on the days she feels stuck and unable to move. And we pray You give her grace and mercy on the days she may stray off course. May she find renewed faith as she sees the growth she can make through each little step.

Galatians 5:25
"If we live by the Spirit, let us also keep in step with the Spirit."

Amen

Day 53
February 22nd

Blessings in Burdens

Lord, tonight we pray for the cowgirl just trying to hold it all together. Between the ranch, the bills, livestock, work, and family she has a lot of irons in the fire. In a cowgirl's day there are so many moving parts, sometimes she's just thankful they don't all run into each other. And on the days they do, she prays for Your grace to see her though. There are times she wishes she had less on her plate, but then she remembers that being busy is a blessing. We pray Lord, that she remembers to pray thanks even when the days are long and hard. We pray Lord, that You hold her steady as she works to hold it all together. And we pray You bring her grace and comfort when it comes apart at the seams. Renew her strength and resilience. May she be a light for You always.

Luke 12:48
"To whom much was given, of him much will be required."

Amen

Day 54
February 23rd

Brokenhearted

Lord, tonight we come to You for the cowgirl seeking healing. It may be physically or emotionally, or it may be for herself or someone she knows. When waiting for healing it's sometimes hard to keep a positive outlook. Sometimes the pain seems endless and then she wonders if there is a purpose in the pain.

Psalm 34:18
"The LORD is near to the brokenhearted and saves the crushed in spirit."

We remind her that she isn't alone in her pain. For You are with her as You guide her to healing. We pray she feels You near and feels Your comfort for healing to come soon.

Amen

Day 55
February 24th

Facing Fears

Lord, tonight we pray for the cowgirl feeling fear. Fear of the unknown, fear of the future, fear of a diagnosis, or fear of things around her she cannot control. The fact is this world has a way of pulling fear out of even the most faith filled. But we pray Lord, You remind us that the fear that is of this world is not from You. May her fears meet the God she knows.

2 Timothy 1:7
"For God hath not given us the spirit of fear; but of power, and of love, and of a sound mind."

We remind her Lord, that power, love and a sound mind are hers to hold and to strengthen her over the fears of this world. We pray she remembers that she doesn't have to control everything around her in order not to fear it. She need only to lay it at Your feet. May she lay her worries into Your healing hands and let her tired mind find rest in You.

Psalm 94:19
"When doubts filled my mind, Your comfort gave me renewed hope."

Amen

Day 56
February 25th

Moving Forward

Lord, tonight we pray for the cowgirl that is trying to move forward. The unfairness of life here on earth has left her a little shaken, a little discouraged, and a little lost. She knows Your plans are greater and she doesn't doubt Your goodness. But the sting that is left on her heart is holding her feet down into the hurt. She prays for guidance and grace when her path gets murky. She prays for strength and mercy when her mind gets stuck. And she prays for healing so that as she puts the pieces back together, she can heal, one piece at a time.

Hebrews 6:3,
"And so, God willing, we will move forward to further understanding."

Amen

Day 57
February 26th

Feeling Heard

Tonight, Lord, we pray for cowgirls that need to feel heard. The world is so loud and full of noise. Noise from the news, social media, the to-do list on the fridge, and all opinions of family or friends. Sometimes she can turn the noise off outside her head, but it just keeps blaring inside her mind. The 'what ifs', 'should haves', and 'maybe I'll find time tomorrows' keep her mind in a constant battle for peace. She just wants to feel like someone is listening and understands. When we look to Your word we see

Psalm 10:17
"You, Lord, hear the desire of the afflicted; you encourage them, and you listen to their prayers."

We pray she takes great comfort to know she is heard and You are near. May she carry that blanket of comfort as she lays her head down tonight and may it quiet the noise.

Amen

Day 58
February 27th

Brave

Lord, tonight we pray for the cowgirl that needs to be brave. Brave enough to step outside her comfort zone. Brave enough to take on a new project, horse, or job. Brave enough to put on a strong face and keep going. Brave enough to face those that don't believe in her and keep trying anyway. We pray for strength in her trials. We pray for peace when her mind races with worry. And we pray she knows that she is never alone in any of those situations. Give her grace and guide her as she steps out in Your strength Lord. May she be bold and brave in Jesus' name.

Joshua 1:9
"Be strong and courageous. Do not be afraid; do not be discouraged, for the LORD your God will be with you wherever you go."

Amen

Day 59
February 28th

A Break

Lord, tonight we pray for the cowgirl that needs a break. A break from the bad news, a break from the heartache, or a break from the tough life lessons. She knows that this world isn't always fair and that things won't always go her way. But that doesn't make the valleys less dark, or the hurt less painful. We pray for comfort and peace in the painful days. We pray for grace on the difficult days. And we pray that she can always feel You near. May she remember that there is light at the end of the darkest valleys as long as she keeps walking. May You be with her every step.

Psalm 34:18
"The LORD is close to the brokenhearted and saves those who are crushed in spirit."

Amen

Day 60
March 1st

Moving Ahead

Lord, we pray for the cowgirl that needs the courage to move. Move her feet, move her mind, move her family, or just move her priorities. She feels like she's in a rut and wants change. But every time she tries to make the move she struggles. We pray she finds courage in You to take the first step.

We pray she knows that with the first step and every step thereafter, You walk with her. No matter the move Lord, we pray she walk in Your will. Guide her with Your grace and direction. We pray she seek You first every morning as she takes the next step.

Proverbs 4:25-27
"Look straight ahead and fix your eyes on what lies before you. Give careful thought to the paths for your feet and be steadfast in all your ways. Don't get sidetracked; keep your feet from following evil."

Amen

Day 61
March 2nd

Passion & Purpose

Lord, tonight we pray for the cowgirl looking to pursue her calling. She has felt You tapping on her heart and nudging her out of her comfort zone. She knows that the passion You have placed in her heart was given to her to serve a purpose. She may not know just how to take the next step, or maybe she isn't sure how to use her passion for Your purpose. We pray Lord, that she listens closely to the whispers in her heart, may she hear Your guidance. We pray she unlock her knees and be willing to move her feet and take the first step towards Your plan. We pray You continue to be her guiding light and open the doors of opportunity. We pray she keeps an open mind and faithful heart to walk through them.

Philippians 2:13
"For God is working in you, giving you the desire and the power in order to fulfill his good purpose."

Amen

Day 62
March 3rd

Joyous Spirit

Lord, tonight we pray for our cowgirl that needs to get her joy back. Piece by piece, she has lost it in the day-to-day trials. We pray Lord, that she leans on You to remind her of the passion and purpose You have put in her heart. Remind her of the joy she feels when she puts that passion to work in Your purpose for her. We pray Lord, that You take away whatever is stealing her joy. May she feel You lift that burden from her heart. May the God of hope fill you with all joy and peace as you trust in him, so that you may overflow with hope by the power of the Holy Spirit.

Romans 15:13.
"Piece by piece may the joy of her days return."

Amen.

Day 63
March 4th

Finding Pause

Tonight, Lord, we pray for the cowgirl that needs to pause. She needs to stop, and just breathe. She needs to take a moment to let her mind and her body catch up to each other. She races each day from one task to the next, never fully taking a moment to find joy in the moment. But we pray Lord, that she remembers that life isn't always about getting to the next goal. Sometimes it's about all the little victories along the way. That is where You are working to build and shape her to be the woman You have called her to be. We pray she takes a moment to embrace the process and opportunities along the way. We pray she find strength and grace in her pause. We pray she takes that moment to renew her faith.

Psalm 61:2
"From the end of the earth I call to You when my heart is faint; Lead me to the rock that is higher than I."

Amen

Day 64
March 5th

Traveling in Grief

Lord, tonight we pray for our cowgirls traveling on a grief journey. It may be new a road for her, or one she's been on for a while. It's not an easy part of her journey and many times it feels lonely. Because no matter the situation, it's different for everyone and though they may try, for some it's just simply hard to relate. We pray she seeks You for refuge when the waves come and she feels like she's drowning in the emotional rollercoaster. And we pray You give her grace when some days are harder to get through than others. And we pray for Your peace and comfort to surround her for each step along the way. May she know she is never alone with You in her heart.

Psalm 34:18,
"The Lord is near to the brokenhearted and saves the crushed in spirit."

Amen

Day 65
March 6th

Journey Direction

Lord, tonight we pray for the cowgirl feeling a little lost on her journey. She knows the ups and downs are to come, but the lefts and rights are a little harder to manage. She even wonders if maybe she's taken a wrong turn somewhere. She sees others making headway and yet she feels like she's just treading water. Tonight, we pray for reassurance, Lord. Just like a GPS is silent for a while when you're on the right path, her path may be long and silent sometimes, but assure her it is indeed the right one. And that when it comes time for the next turn, You will open that door of opportunity. Her promise to You Lord, is that she will walk through it, so give her the confidence to do so.

Philippians 1:6
"And I am certain that God, who began the good work within you, will continue his work until it is finally finished on the day when Christ Jesus returns."

Amen

Day 66
March 7th

Fresh Outlook

Lord, we come to You for the cowgirl whose spring isn't going as planned. She was so ready for warmer weather and all the goals she had set. But so far, the downs seem to outweigh the ups and she is starting to get discouraged. We pray Lord, that she remembers nothing worth having comes easy and everything she is working towards is a process. We pray tomorrow she wakes with a fresh new day and a clean slate in mind. We pray she wakes with You in her heart with renewed confidence in Your plan for her lifting her wings and her spirits.

Hebrews 12:2
"We do this by keeping our eyes on Jesus, the champion who initiates and perfects our faith."

Amen

Day 67
March 8th

Rough Road

Lord, tonight we pray for the cowgirl that has hit a rough patch in the road. The journey ahead is full of big dreams and goals, and yet she seems to be finding a lot of potholes lately. She is trying hard to stay tough through the trouble but sometimes she feels the discouragement set it. So, we pray for peace and comfort when the frustration boils over and down her cheeks. We pray she takes pause to see You moving in her mess and bringing clarity to her chaos. It may be hard to see through the tears Lord, but we pray she sees You. May she see You in the little things that bring a smile. May she see You in the helping hands of others. And may she pause long enough to realize that she is never truly alone or lost. You are with her all along and You will see her through to smoother roads, one step at a time.

Isaiah 41:10
"Don't be afraid, for I am with you. Don't be discouraged, for I am your God. I will strengthen you and help you. I will hold you up with my victorious right hand."

Amen

Day 68
March 9th

Capable Cowgirl

Tonight, we pray for the cowgirl that needs to be reminded she is capable. Capable of what You have called her to do. Between work, her home, her kids, her family, and her animals her plate is full of blessings. But sometimes blessings overflow and feel overwhelming. She wonders if she's making the right business decisions and spending enough time with the kids. Or if she just had more time to clean up, cook, or organize she would feel better. But the truth is, Lord, she is capable, and she is equipped to be all You have called her to be. We pray You remind her that she is an imperfect soul loved by a perfect God. We pray Lord, that you remind her that on the days she doesn't feel strong enough, she finds strength in You. On the days she feels lost, she seeks You for guidance. And on the days she doesn't feel capable, we pray You remind her of Your word.

Proverbs 31:29
"There are many virtuous and capable women in the world, but you surpass them all!"

May she feel those words sink into her soul. And may she remember she was,

"created for such a time as this" -Esther 4:14.

Amen

Day 69
March 10th

New Opportunities

Lord, tonight we pray for the cowgirl looking forward to the new year. She is ready for spring and all the opportunities it brings with it. She prays for guidance as she prepares and makes her goals for the coming year. She prays that as she follows that purpose You put in her heart, she would accept the doors that close and walk through the open ones. We pray for grace and mercy as she navigates the highs and lows of the journey ahead. We pray she takes the lessons from her past and learns how to progress through them in the future. May she find joy along the way.

Psalm 119:105
"Your word is a lamp to my feet and a light to my path."

Amen

Day 70
March 11th

Cowgirl Tribe

Lord, tonight we pray for the cowgirl that misses her tribe. The ones that she grew up rodeoing or showing with, but life has taken them different directions and to different states. The ones that she stood in the rain, mud, and 110 heat-index with. The ones that stayed up till 2am to video your slack run or sat shotgun on a late-night drive. The ones she doesn't see or talk to for months but picks right back up whenever they left off. We pray thanks over all those memories she holds so dear, the inside jokes and late-night trailer talk about grown up life. The ones that dried her tears and prayed to You when life got hard. We pray thanks for these lifelong friends You have provided Lord, for we know it's Your hand that molded these friendships. Although we don't see them often enough, we pray they know she is always just a phone call away. And we pray for Your hand of protection over them always.

1 Thessalonians 5:11
"Therefore encourage one another and build one another up, just as you are doing."

Amen

Day 71
March 12th

Cowgirl Projects

Lord, tonight we come to You for the cowgirl with projects. She may be building fence, a barn, a house, or just mending any or all of those, Lord. A cowgirl's projects are never really done, Lord, because You know as soon as one is finished, she will find another (or another finds her...). Some of these days are full of accomplishment, but others leave her a bit defeated, Lord. We ask You to meet her there, meet her right where she is, Lord. Hold her tired arms steady as she swings the hammer to mend the fence at 1am. Comfort and dry her tears as she gets a tough report at the vet. You made her tough and resilient in all circumstances, Lord, but tonight we ask to lay it all at Your feet. We know the projects will still be there in the morning, but tonight when she lays her head on her pillow let her find rest in You.

Ecclesiastes 3:1
"There is a time for everything, and a season for every activity under the heavens"

Amen

Day 72
March 13th

Surrender Burdens

Lord, tonight we come to You to pray for the cowgirl trying to play catch-up. She's been running around burning the candle at both ends and she feels burnt out. So many moving parts rely on her throughout the day, she doesn't feel like she can let her guard down without it all coming crashing down around her. We pray Lord, for her to seek You for peace and balance. We pray she find direction and guidance through You to navigate the hectic days ahead. May she surrender the worry and stress that comes with it. May she lay it at Your feet.

Psalm 94:19
"When anxiety was great within me, Your comfort gave me renewed hope and cheer."

Amen

Day 73
March 14th

Thankful Opportunities

Lord, tonight we pray for the cowgirl thankful for the journey. Thankful for the opportunities ahead of her, and thankful for the lessons behind her. We pray she thanks You as much in the lows as she does in the highs. We pray she remembers that each step, even and especially the difficult ones, has led her to her successes. When those difficult steps come, we pray she remembers they are all part of the journey. May she find joy in each piece of the journey. We pray You guide her steps and bring her peace along the way.

2 Peter 3:9
"The Lord is not slow to fulfill His promise as some count slowness, but is patient toward you."

Amen

Day 74
March 15th

New Beginnings

Lord, tonight we pray for the cowgirl beginning something new. It may be a new job, a new barn, a new horse, or a new home. Changes can be exciting and overwhelming no matter the circumstances. We pray for courage and strength as she takes on the opportunities along her journey. We pray for perseverance whenever the journey gets tough. And we pray for guidance as she steps into the unknown. May she seek Your will and direction in all she does.

Jeremiah 29:11
"For I know the plans I have for you," declares the LORD, "plans to prosper you and not to harm you, plans to give you hope and a future."

Amen

Day 75
March 16th

Built on Blessings

Dear Lord, tonight we pray for the cowgirl's family. The ones who helped her fall in love with her first pony, took her to her first rodeo or simply encouraged her to chase after her "horse crazy" dreams! May they know that all the sacrifices and time dedicated has been well spent. What better way to teach of Your love than in the saddle or at the barn. We pray they know how much the long nights and early mornings meant, and we pray blessing over each of them.

Colossians 2:7
"Let your roots grow down into him, and let your lives be built on him. Then your faith will grow strong in the truth you were taught, and you will overflow with thankfulness."

Amen

Day 76
March 17th

Guide Our Steps

Lord, tonight we pray for the cowgirl that needs to find joy in the journey. She needs to throw a log on the fire that burns within her. The road may be bumpy, but it's still a blessing. We pray she sees all the little victories on the road she travels. We pray when she feels lost that she turns to You to guide her path. Restore her faith and give her grace. Renew the passion in her heart that has brought her to where she is now. We pray that she see You move in her life even when things go different than she has planned. Bring her peace and guide her steps so that she may see joy in each one.

1 Peter 1:6
"There is wonderful joy ahead, even though you must endure trials for a little while."

Amen

Day 77
March 18th

Forgiveness

Lord, tonight we pray for the cowgirl working on forgiveness. She may be working to forgive a friend or family member. Or maybe she is working to forgive herself. The thing about forgiveness is that when it's withheld it always hurts the one holding it more than the one it's withheld from. We pray she can find the peace of letting go. We pray no matter the reason for forgiveness that she seeks your guidance to let go and forgive. We pray You cover her in the peace that passes all understanding as she does so Lord. We pray You free her from the chains that tie her down.

Mark 11:25
"And when you stand praying, if you hold anything against anyone, forgive them"

Amen

Day 78
March 19th

Fresh Start

Lord, tonight we pray for the cowgirl that needs a good sleep to wash away the troubles of the day. Rest to renew her faith and recharge her spirit. She needs a fresh start to a day with a new outlook. She may just be in a rough patch, or just run out of patience. Maybe she's in a season of waiting and her mind has grown a bit tired. Whatever the case may be, Lord, we know You are there and will see her through.

Lamentations 3:22-23
"Because of the Lord's great love we are not consumed, for His compassions never fail. They are new every morning; great is your faithfulness."

May she rise in the morning refreshed and ready for the journey You have placed her on. Give her strength and courage to face the new day.

Amen

Day 79
March 20th

Old Soul

Tonight, we pray for the cowgirl caring for an older horse, Lord. Day in and day out, she tediously nurtures the old soul that has given so many years to the humans in their life. She knows any day may be the last day. So, without complaint, she wets the grain/hay, spreads the fresh bedding, mixes the supplements, and kisses that sweet grey face. This winter has been especially hard, Lord. Give her strength and comfort as she longs for warmer days for her old friend. And give her peace in knowing that You see her and know she is doing her best. And when the day comes that she must give him back to You, may she smile through the tears as she remembers the wonderful years they spent together.

1 Peter 4:10
"Each of you should use whatever gift you have received to serve others, as faithful stewards of God's grace in its various forms."

Amen

Day 80
March 21st

Grace and Answered Prayer

Tonight, Lord, we pray for the cowgirl that feels like she is spinning her wheels. So much drive and determination burning inside of her, and she isn't sure which way is the right way to go. She prays and looks for answers and then feels discouraged when the door closes. She knows You have a plan and a path for her, and she knows it exceeds all she dreams herself, but she feels like she can't find the path. Is this just a valley of darkness? A season of waiting? Or did she take a wrong turn somewhere? Her mind races with so many questions and she begs for the answers. We pray Lord, You give her grace as she feels the impatience creep in. We pray You give her peace to remember You are in control and she can count on Your promises. And we pray You give her the direction and the clarity she seeks. May she find comfort in Your word.

Proverbs 3: 5-6
"Trust in the Lord with all your heart and lean not on your own understanding; in all your ways submit to him, and he will make your paths straight."

Amen

Day 81
March 22nd

Feeling Defeated

Lord, tonight we come to You to pray for our cowgirl feeling defeated. She works, and prays, and gives all she has and still feels like it isn't enough, or she can't get ahead. It feels like two steps forward and one step back, Lord. We pray You lift up her weary head, You breathe life and love back into her sails, and remind her that You're not done with her yet! This world is unkind and unfair, but she is the daughter of the King, and we pray she looks into the mirror and remembers that nothing is impossible with You and through You. Her strength may fail her, but Yours never will. So, for as long as You live in her heart, Lord, may she remember that she can do all through You who strengthens her.

1 Timothy 6:12
"Fight the good fight for the true faith. Hold tightly to the eternal life to which God has called you."

Amen

Day 82
March 23rd

Relationship with Christ

Lord, tonight we pray for the cowgirls seeking out the next step in their relationship with You. They may have just asked You into their hearts for the first time and they aren't sure what to do now. Maybe they're looking to grow in their prayer relationship, Lord. Or maybe she feels the push to go out and do Your will, to be Your hands and feet, but she's not sure how to go about it. All these cowgirls are seeking You, Lord, and we pray no matter how different, that You meet them right where they are. May they feel Your peace and direction for the way they should move. May they feel Your peace and grace wash over them to start their new life in You, Lord. May they feel at ease to drop to their knees and call out to You as the Lord of her life. And may they step out in faith knowing that as long as they look to walk for You, that You will guide her every step. We ask all of this in Your precious and Holy name.

Jeremiah 29:13
"You will seek me and find me when you seek me with all your heart."

Amen

Day 83
March 24th

Finding Fulfillment

Lord, tonight we pray for the cowgirl that is feeling unfulfilled. She has worked and prepared for the goals, dreams, plans, and purpose You have put in her heart, and now she needs to go live it. She needs to "put her money where her mouth is" so to speak and go after what makes her happy. A cowgirl feeling unfulfilled is just a cowgirl that hasn't listened to the purpose You designed her for. Sometimes she finds herself making excuses and taking the easy way out. Maybe it's not the right time, or she doesn't feel ready. But the truth is, You designed her for this very moment and very time. Whatever the situation Lord, we pray she remembers that push she feels in her heart is You and the calling You have for her. We pray she realizes that longing in her soul that stings as she watches others push past their fears is just a reminder of what she knows she is capable of. Give her strength and courage and grace as she takes each step in the journey ahead towards fulfillment.

Esther 4:14
"Perhaps you were created for such a time as this."

Amen

Day 84
March 25th

Grace

Lord tonight we pray for our cowgirls that seek Your grace. Life pulls so many directions Lord, that sometimes she feels like she is coming apart at the seams. Her temper gets shorter, as the to-do list gets longer. She feels like she's failing at keeping up with all life throws at her, and she needs your forgiveness and grace to pull her through.

2 Corinthians 12:9
"But He said to me, '"My grace is sufficient for you, for my power is made perfect in weakness."' Therefore, I will boast all the more gladly about my weaknesses, so that Christ's power may rest on me."

We pray Lord, as she seeks You she will lay her weakness in Your hands and allow Your power to take over. May she feel Your grace cover her and take away her insecurities. May she know and feel You are in control, and may she find comfort.

Amen

Day 85
March 26th

Soft Heart

Lord, tonight we pray for the cowgirl with a soft heart. She feels things more deeply than most. She feels the troubles of others, her animals, and the world and they weigh heavily on her own heart. She finds herself taking on the weight of the world and looking for ways to fix all the brokenness around her. We pray Lord, that she remembers that You are the healer of the world, and the burden does not rest on her shoulders. We pray she turn her worries into prayers and let them rest with You. We pray for comfort and peace for her soft heart. Bring her rest in knowing You are in control and her prayers are heard.

1Peter 3:4
"It should consist of what is inside the heart with the imperishable quality of a gentle and quiet spirit, which is very valuable in God's eyes."

Amen

Day 86
March 27th

"Give You Rest"

Lord, tonight we pray for the cowgirl that needs to catch a break. It feels like lately if it's not one thing it's another. From equipment breaking to sick kiddos or livestock, she just jumps from one mess to another. The messes overflow to the finances and that strains other relationships and this cowgirl's heart needs a place to rest. When we look to Your word Lord, we find rest.

Matthew 11:28
"Come to Me, all who are weary and burdened, and I will give you rest."

We pray she comes to You to lay her heavy heart and finds rest.

Amen

Day 87
March 28th

Finding Peace in Anxiety

Lord, tonight we pray for the cowgirl with anxiety. She hides it well, behind a tough exterior and a pretty smile. She works around it and through it because that's what cowgirls do. But somedays it sneaks up and steals her joy. Somedays her smile fades and she needs Your strength and grace to help her go on. We pray she seeks You and the peace You provide. May You calm her racing mind and bring peace to the storm that brews under the surface.

Philippians 4:6-7
"Do not be anxious about anything, but in every situation, by prayer and petition, with thanksgiving, present your requests to God. And the peace of God, which transcends all understanding, will guard your hearts and your minds in Christ Jesus."

Amen

Day 88
March 29th

God's Plan

Lord, tonight we pray for the cowgirl that needs to have faith in your plan. She dreams her dreams and pushes toward those goals and plans she has Lord, but sometimes they seem just out of reach. She's a bit impatient when it comes to waiting, even when she knows Your timing is always the right timing. We ask You tonight to scoop up those dreams and plans Lord and remind her that YOU have got this and she is not alone on this journey. And that the dreams and plans You have for her are far greater than she could ever dream or plan on her own. Deep down she knows this Lord, because she's watched You work it in her life over and over. Forgive her impatience Lord and remind her to trust and have faith.

Habakkuk 2:3
"For still the vision awaits its appointed time; it hastens to the end—it will not lie. If it seems slow, wait for it; it will surely come; it will not delay."

Amen

Day 89
March 30th

Quiet Faithfulness

Tonight, Lord we pray for the cowgirl that needs quiet. She needs quiet in her mind, and she needs the craziness around her to just quiet. It's amazing how loud the thoughts in her own head can get, so she prays for You to settle the noise. Push out the distractions and the negativity. Bring light and truth to settle her mind. This world is so full of noise-opinions flying around her from all directions. And no matter how many she hears, somehow, they all tell her she is doing something wrong or how she is somehow not enough. We pray Lord, that You would cover her ears and eyes to the things that are not good for her. Shield and guard her heart from all the noise. May she rise up from all of it and find her peace in You.

Philippians 4:7
"And the Peace of God, which transcends all understanding, will guard your hearts and your minds in Christ Jesus."

Amen

Day 90
March 31st

Patience in His Plan

Lord, tonight we pray for the cowgirl that needs to take it one step at a time. She's longing to run and and fly and chase the passion You have laid in her heart. She knows the road won't be easy, but she's ready and willing to take it all in stride. But patience pays off, and faith in Your plan provides strength. We pray she remembers that just as a vinedresser that prepares vines to bear much fruit, that You Lord, are also preparing her for the journey ahead. We pray that even as she anxiously anticipates the journey ahead, that she remembers to take it one step at a time. We pray she remembers to follow Your lead and seek Your direction. For when she follows the pace You set for her Lord, You will sustain her.

Isaiah 40:31
"But those who hope in the Lord will renew their strength. They will soar on wings like eagles; they will run and not grow weary; they will walk and not be faint."

Amen

Day 91
April 1st

Lay it at His Feet

Lord, tonight we pray for the cowgirl with the weight of the world on her shoulders. She wears many hats and has too many irons in the fire to count. She is the keeper of all things and feels like the master of none. She is the glue that holds it all together, but somedays she feels like she is one thread away from coming undone. We pray Lord, that she remembers to lay those burdens at Your feet. We pray she remembers that when she feels like she is falling apart, You hold all the pieces of her together. We pray for grace and mercy on the days that are too much. May she find comfort and a place to land in Your word. We pray she take a moment to breathe and feel Your peace wash over her, guide her steps piece by piece. one step at a time.

Mathew 11:28-30
"Come to Me, all of you who are weary and carry heavy burdens, and I will give you rest. Take My yoke upon you and learn from Me, for I am gentle and humble in heart, and you will find rest for your souls. For My yoke is easy, and My burden is light."

Amen

Day 92
April 2nd

Making a way

Lord, we pray for our cowgirls needing You to move mountains. She needs You to do what others say is impossible. Her faith in You is strong Lord, and she knows You are her only answer to her biggest obstacle.

Isaiah 40:4
"Every valley shall be lifted up, and every mountain and hill be made low; the uneven ground shall become level, and the rough places a plain."

This scripture tells her that You can take anything in her path and make it possible for her to navigate with You in her heart. May she hold that truth in her heart as she prays for Your guidance and help along her path.

Amen

Day 93
April 3rd

Rock in Turbulent Seas

Lord, tonight we pray for the cowgirl that needs comfort. She works hard and puts on a brave face, but sometimes she just needs a soft place to land. She feels Your blessings all around and yet sometimes her stresses and worries still bubble over and run down her cheeks. We pray You bring her the peace that passes all understanding. Cover her in a blanket of Your unconditional love. We pray when she feels like no one is listening, she knows You hear her heart. May she find peace in Your grace, and she pours her heart out to You.

Psalm 61:2
"From the end of the earth I will cry to You whenever my heart is overwhelmed. Lead me to the towering rock of safety."

Amen

Day 94
April 4th

Light in Darkness

Lord, tonight we pray for our cowgirls that are discouraged. Discouraged about the path they are on, the choices they have made, or the obstacles in their path. They know that life is full of hills and valleys, moments of brilliance and moments of darkness. But recently she feels stuck in a valley of darkness. She wonders if she should throw in the towel and try something different all together. Sometimes change can be good and, Lord, if it is change she needs, we pray You guide her steps to get there. But if it's Your will that she stay the course, Lord, we pray You meet her there also. We pray You lift her head and straighten her crown and remind her she is a daughter of the King and through You nothing is impossible.

Isaiah 41:10
"Fear not, for I am with you; be not dismayed, for I am your God; I will strengthen you, I will help you, I will uphold you with my righteous right hand."

Amen

Day 95
April 5th

Rodeo Dream

Lord, tonight we pray for the cowgirl chasing the rodeo dream. She may be trying the new breakaway pro rodeo dream or maybe she's a tried-and-true barrel racer still chasing those white lines. Maybe it's our Jr., H.S. or collegiate girls looking at making the trip to nationals in the next couple months. Whatever the dream Lord, the one You have put in her heart, we pray You see it through. We pray she feel the peace only You can give as the announcer calls her name. We pray she lays her confidence in You and the talents You have given her and the hard work she has put in. But most of all Lord, at the end of the day, win or learn, we pray she takes pause to look to You and give You the thanks. We pray she gives You the glory and shines a light for You.

Philippians 4:6
"Do not be anxious about anything, but in every situation, by prayer and petition, with thanksgiving, present your requests to God."

Amen

Day 96
April 6th

Long Term Goals

Tonight, Lord, we pray for the cowgirl working through a long-term goal. The highs and the lows. The long nights. The early mornings. Blood, sweat, and tears through each struggle. She has found joy in the journey and prayed her way through the valleys. We pray for strength as she continues to navigate her path. We pray for grace and mercy for her short-comings and doubts. We pray she feels you near on the days she feels alone. May she find patience when the road gets long and remember Your timing, not her own.

Proverbs 16:9
"A man's heart plans his course, but the LORD determines his steps."

Amen

Day 97
April 7th

Servants Heart

Lord, tonight we pray for the cowgirl that has too much on her plate. She wears many hats and balances a heavy load on her shoulders. She isn't good at saying no and most days you wouldn't notice the toll it takes on her. She's afraid if she doesn't help someone out when they ask that she let them down. We pray Lord, she realizes it's ok to set healthy boundaries and that although You gave her a servant's heart, she need not run herself into dust trying to make every piece fit for everyone. We pray she understands that quality is better than quantity, and that being spread too thin doesn't really help anyone. We pray You give her peace in her heart to give where she can and take care of herself too. A servant's heart is a great gift, and we pray blessings over all she does.

Ephesians 6:7
"Serve wholeheartedly, as if you were serving the Lord, not people."

Amen

Day 98
April 8th

Turn to God

Lord, tonight we pray for the cowgirl that feels like she is backed into a corner. Due to choice or circumstance, she has found herself in a situation that has left her feeling like there is nowhere to turn. Her back is against a wall, and she isn't sure what she should do next. Lord, we pray You bring her clarity, we pray You sweep away the clutter in her mind and in her life. Take away the blinders this world has put on her eyes and let her see Your love and Your truth. We pray Lord, You show her and guide her to the journey and plan You have for her. We pray she understands that it may not be easy, but we pray she remembers she is never alone with You in her heart. Be her guide, be her comfort, and be her peace.

Isaiah 45:22
"Turn to Me and be saved, all the ends of the earth; For I am God, and there is no other."

Amen

Day 99
April 9th

Ready for a Comeback

Tonight, we pray for the cowgirl who's ready to turn her setback into a comeback. She's had a rough go, perhaps in a valley of lows, or on the bottom side of that roller coaster of life. But you can't keep a cowgirl down for long, she's the type that learns from this and she's ready to come back stronger. She's taking the time of waiting in her setback to make a game plan, to prepare for the comeback she will make. She knows that just as a vinedresser prepares the vine to bear much fruit, you, too, are preparing her for greatness. We pray Lord, that she seeks You and Your timing so that she may find the road to success.

Romans 3: 5:7
"We also glory in our troubles, because we know that troubles produce perseverance; perseverance, character; and character, hope. And hope does not put us to shame, because God's love has been poured out into our hearts through the Holy Spirit, who has been given to us."

Amen

Day 100
April 10th

Stay the Course

Lord, tonight we pray for our cowgirls that are in the middle of the grind. That dirt road that's longer with more potholes and a few extra valleys. This is her journey Lord, and the path You have asked her to walk and so she does so with courage. But sometimes she sees the highlight reel of the highway or those that have taken the short cuts and she wonders if maybe she took a wrong turn. We pray You breathe life into her lungs and strength into her heart to keep charging through. We pray You remind her that her journey is as unique as the reward You have ahead for her. Refresh her memory of Your promises for a better future. We pray Lord, she seeks Your guidance and grace when the road gets rough. May she be steadfast and strong towards the goal You have set in front of her and may she hang tightly to Your word every step of the way.

Philippians 1:6
"I am sure of this, that He who started a good work in You will carry it on to completion until the day of Christ Jesus."

Amen

Day 101
April 11th

Find Refuge

Lord, tonight we pray for the cowgirls that find themselves in a moment of fear. Fear of the future, fear of the unknown, fear of the journey You have asked her to walk. As cowgirls Lord, fear isn't something she is used to feeling, and even when she does, she finds ways to brush it off. But this feels different Lord, this one has grabbed ahold of her heart and isn't letting go. So, we pray Lord, for You to speak truth into her soul. Remind her that fear is a liar and that You are the way, the truth, and the light. We pray You find the hurt and fear deep within her and heal it, Lord. We pray You cast out the doubts and strengthen her faith. May she remember that even in the toughest season, she is never alone. And no road You ask her to walk will be in vain.

Psalm 91:4-5
"He will cover you with his feathers, and under his wings you will find refuge; His faithful promises are your armor and protection. You will not fear the terror of night, nor the arrow that flies by day. "

Amen

Day 102
April 12th

Outside the Comfort Zone

Lord, tonight we pray for the cowgirl trying to get comfortable with the uncomfortable. She is seeking Your plan and she knows Your plans are going to take her outside her comfort zone. She knows if she wants things she's never had, she will have to do things she's never done. She knows she is going to have to trust in You and forge her way with her mustard seed of faith. We pray You bring her strength in the journey ahead. We pray she learn through the growing pains and find perseverance and strength she didn't know she had. And through every step Lord, we pray she seeks to glorify You. May she shine Your light even on her darkest days, and may she praise You in every step.

Psalm 73:26
"My flesh and my heart may fail, but God is the strength of my heart and my portion forever."

Amen

Day 103
April 13th

Restore Joy

Lord, tonight we pray for the cowgirl struggling to find joy in the journey. The tough breaks, disappointments and unmet expectations have hit pretty deep. She flashes a smile and positive words to be a light for others and hopes it sinks inward. She knows Your love abounds around her and knows Your plans are good, but right now her heart hurts. Her faith feels a bit rattled, and we pray she seeks You to restore it. We pray You give her the grace and mercy she needs in those moments of weakness. We pray she remembers that You hold her heart even in the broken parts. May she remember You are in every step of her journey and the best is yet to come. She need only to trust in You. Restore her, uplift her, and give her Your peace, Lord.

Psalm 71:20
"Though You have shown me troubles and misfortunes, You will revive me once again. Even from the depths of the earth, You will bring me back up."

Amen

Day 104
April 14th

Stronger Relationship

Lord tonight we want to pray for those cowgirls seeking You. Some may have just asked You into their hearts and some may have done so a long time ago but have strayed from Your path lately. And some may not know You in their hearts Lord but find themselves reading this post. This is for all of those cowgirl hearts needing You to fill them with the peace and joy only a relationship with You can provide. We pray they open that door to their hearts and ask You to surround them in Your love. You have the love and forgiveness for each and every one. We praise You for the souls You have saved and those on their way to salvation through You, Lord.

Ephesians 3:19
"To know the love of Christ that surpasses knowledge, that you may be filled with all the fullness of God."

Amen

Day 105
April 15th

Never Alone

Lord, tonight we pray for our cowgirl that feels alone. It may be in a relationship, her job, or a situation. She may feel distanced from You, maybe her prayer life isn't what it used to be, or maybe she isn't sure how to start one. Sometimes she feels like she has no one to turn to or relate to in her troubles. Lord, we pray she remembers that prayer doesn't always need to be formal, that she can close her eyes and come to You anywhere. In a field, in the barn, in a cubicle, or just sitting a parked car. Because she is never alone, she is only ever a prayer away from the most understanding ear. We pray tonight she closes her eyes and comes to You and finds the peace that comes with Your presence. May her soul feel Your embrace and find comfort in You.

Matthew 28:20
"And remember, I am with you always, to the end of the age."

Amen

Day 106
April 16th

Stepping out in Faith

Lord, tonight we pray for the cowgirl that is stepping out on faith. Taking a leap into something new. Maybe headfirst or maybe just dipping in her toes. This step out may have excitement or a little bit of fear. New challenges often do, and she knows it's You in which she will find her strength to move forward. We pray You give her peace in the moments of uncertainty. We pray You bring her grace for the steps that won't come easy. Give her courage to press onward to the plan You have for her. And we pray she find joy in the journey. 2

Corinthians 5:7
"For we walk by faith, not by sight."

Amen

Day 107
April 17th

Wait on the Lord

Lord, we pray for our cowgirls that have plans. Big plans or little plans. Plans for their career, plans for their horses, or plans for their family and future. Their plans are driven with the purpose and passion You have put in their hearts and they long to see them through. We pray Lord, that they remember all good things come in Your timing, not theirs. We pray they realize that just as carefully as He prepared the earth to bear fruit, He too is preparing them for the plans laid on their hearts. We pray You bring them patience and guide them to develop into the cowgirl You have planned for them to be. May they wait on You and Your timing and find comfort in Your plans for them.

Isaiah 40:31.
"For those who wait on the Lord will renew their strength and soar on wings like eagles, they will walk and not grow weary, they will run and not be faint."

Amen

Day 108
April 18th

From Our hands to Yours

We come to you tonight, Lord, to pray for the cowgirl in heartache. It's spring Lord, and that means the miracle of new life. What a joy and a blessing it is to be a part of bringing that new life into this world. But you know it doesn't come without heartache, Lord. All year long she pours her heart into the mares, cows, ewes, does, and other mommas to help them nourish the precious gifts they are growing. But sometimes there is just nothing that can be done and she's left in tears holding lifelessness in her hands. Only You know why some of these blessings aren't meant to be, and we pray for You to bring peace to our hearts for these situations. We pray You give us comfort in knowing that when they leave our hands they are welcomed by Yours.

Psalm 31:14-15
"But I trust in You, O Lord: I say, 'You are my God.' My times are in Your hands."

Amen

Day 109
April 19th

Stuck in the Middle

Lord, tonight we pray for the cowgirl that feels stuck in the middle. It may be stuck between leaving someone or something or staying. Maybe she's stuck between a choice of careers. Or maybe she feels stuck between family that doesn't get along. Whatever the case, Lord, we pray that she seeks You for guidance. We pray You fill her with peace and comfort when the pressure feels too much. We pray she knows that You are with her no matter the situation even when it feels lonely. Give her grace as she works her way through the middle Lord and give guidance for her words and actions.

Philippians 4:12
"I know what it is to be in need, and I know what it is to have plenty. I have learned the secret of being content in any and every situation, whether well fed or hungry, whether living in plenty or in want."

Amen

Day 110
April 20th

Refreshed and Replenished

Lord tonight we pray for the cowgirl with new beginnings. It may be a new job, a new home, a new baby, a new relationship, or a new horse. No matter the situation, Lord, we pray thanks over the opportunities ahead. She finds herself a mix of emotions, excitement, anticipation, and a little bit of nerves. She prays for Your guidance as she embarks down this new path, Lord. And we know the journey won't always be smooth Lord, so we pray for Your wisdom, mercy, and peace to wash over her as she navigates the bumps in the road. May she find Your grace and joy in this new journey. Watch over her, guide her and bless her. May she return all the glory and thanks to You, Lord.

Lamentations 3:23
"Great is his faithfulness; his mercies begin afresh each morning."

Amen

Day 111
April 21st

God's Grace

Lord, tonight we pray for the cowgirl that is anxious, worried, and in need of Your peace. The peace that passes all understanding. In the moments where everything feels out of her control, we pray for You to take control. We pray You take control of the situations and things that bring the worry, Lord. We pray she remembers the even when the journey feels difficult, You will guide her steps. May You cover her in Your grace and mercy. May she feel Your strength surround her and empower her, mind, body and soul.

Luke 12:25
"And which of you by being anxious can add a single hour to his span of life?"

Amen

Day 112
April 22nd

Perspective

Lord, tonight we pray for the cowgirl that needs to take a step back, seek You, and thank You. The hustle and bustle of life can sometimes get the best of her, and she forgets to see the bigger picture. She can get caught up in the grind and the drive behind it. She needs a reminder to pause and look to the One who put the passion in her heart and gave her the talent in the first place. We pray Lord, that she take a breath and pause to give You the glory and the thanks for all she has and all she does. May she seek Your grace and seek to do Your will. As her life fills with blessings, may she take reflection and let You be her guide in all she does.

Luke 12:48
"To whom much is given, much will be required."

Amen

Day 113
April 23rd

Cowgirl Up

Lord, tonight we pray for the cowgirl that needs to cowgirl up. She needs to pull up her big girl britches and deal with some things she's been putting off. This world has thrown her a fair share of tough breaks and heartaches, but she knows she has to move forward. We pray Lord, that she knows You see her struggle and hear her cries and that You have been beside her all this time. We pray she remembers her feelings are valid and it's ok to feel them, but it's not ok to unpack her bags and live there. You did not create her to give up or give in,

2 Timothy 1:7
"You have given her a spirit of power, love, and a sound mind. May she look to You for her guidance and strength to see her to the other side."

Amen

Day 114
April 24th

Well Done

Lord, tonight we pray for the cowgirl that feels like she's not enough. Not mom enough, cowgirl enough, housekeeper enough, loving enough, or ranchy enough. Different tasks throughout the day seem to find her insecurities and she feels like she comes up short. She looks around her and feels like someone else is always just a little bit better. We remind her Lord, that we are the BODY of Christ, all created with our own purpose and our own unique talents. Remind her that just as the human body has different parts that each have different roles, so does the body of Christ. We pray she remembers the talents and purpose You have blessed her with. We pray she finds that she is most definitely enough for each purpose You have called her to. May she continue to pursue the passion that You have placed in her heart to work towards Your purpose for her. And that one day she will hear the words of Mathew.

Mathew 25:23
"Well done my good and faithful servant."

Amen

Day 115
April 25th

Turn off your Worries

Lord, tonight we pray for those cowgirls needing to give their worries to You. It may be big things weighing on her mind, or a dozen little things tugging at her heart. She trusts Your plan and knows she shouldn't worry, yet she finds herself in the busy of her mind distracted with the what-ifs. We pray you give her strength to really and truly give it all to You. Because no matter how hard she holds those worries inside, the true peace only comes from turning them over to You. We pray she lays them at Your feet Lord, with confidence and trust in the peace it will bring her heart.

Philippians 4:6-7
"Do not be anxious about anything, but in every situation, by prayer and petition, with thanksgiving, present your requests to God. And the peace of God, which transcends all understanding, will guard your hearts and your minds in Christ Jesus."

Amen

Day 116
April 26th

Move Those Feet

Tonight, Lord, we pray for the cowgirl seeking Your guidance but too afraid to take the steps. She knows Your path is better, she knows You are with her if only she would move her feet. It seemed so easy to follow a path laid out in front of her, until she realized she doesn't know all the steps and she isn't in control. We pray Lord, that she turn over control to You by being brave enough to make that first step. We pray she finds the strength to put her faith in Your plan. May she be reminded of Your faithfulness and step out into Your plan for her and move those feet!

Proverbs 16:9:
"We can make our plans, but the Lord determines our steps."

Amen

Day 117
April 27th

Calm the Chaos

Lord, tonight we pray for the cowgirl facing uncertainty. She has grown accustomed to the roller coaster of the journey she is on and looks to You for guidance. Through every triumph and trial You have guided her steps and given her grace. However, she has yet to get a grasp on the anxiety of the uncertainty of what lies ahead of her. Will it be a triumph, or yet another trial? Maybe she's waiting for results from the Dr. or the vet. Perhaps she's waiting for a phone call about a job or new home. Whatever the situation we pray for peace as she waits out the uncertainty. May she also find peace in the outcome, knowing that You are with her, and Your plan will prevail. Give her grace and strength as she navigates the days ahead.

2 Corinthians 1:3-4
"Blessed be the God and Father of our Lord Jesus Christ, the Father of mercies and God of all comfort, who comforts us in all our affliction."

Amen

Day 118
April 28th

Matters of the Heart

Lord, tonight we pray for the cowgirl with a hurt heart. She may be hiding it and not really ready to share with others. We pray Lord, she gives it to You. We pray You hold her tender heart in Your hands and cover her in comfort. It may be the kind of hurt that passes with time, or it may be the kind she carries for a lifetime. If it's a passing hurt Lord, we pray You let the time move quickly and bring healing. If it's one that she will carry Lord, we pray she knows You will carry the hurt with her and she will never be alone with it.

Psalm 34:18
"The Lord is near to the brokenhearted and saves the crushed in spirit."

Amen

Day 119
April 29th

Find Rest

Lord, tonight we pray for the cowgirl needing rest. Mentally, physically, or emotionally. She runs on empty most days just trying to keep her head above water. Running errands and fixing problems are the things that fill her days. The selfish world around her makes her servant's heart hurt. She prays for Your presence to bring peace to the chaos around her. She prays for rest for the worries that fill her mind. And she prays for guidance to navigate the obstacles in her days. Jesus says, "Come to me, all of you who are weary and carry heavy burdens, and I will give you rest. Take my yoke upon you. Let me teach you, because I am humble and gentle at heart, and you will give rest for your souls. For My yoke is easy to bear, and the burden I give you is light.

Matthew 11 28-30
"May she feel Your peace and find rest tonight."

Amen

Day 120
April 30th

Doubt

Lord, tonight we pray for the cowgirl that is doubting. Doubting herself, her abilities, her situation. But if You asked her if she doubted You Lord, she would reply with, "Well of course not!" To that we say, then why would you doubt yourself or anything about it?! Because the Lord himself made you and his plans for you. He gave you your talents, gifts, hopes and dreams. And He has guided you to this very point, so what is there to doubt? If you don't doubt the Lord, then you can't doubt yourself or this journey you're on. We pray she reads that over and over until it sinks in. We pray she takes a moment to realize that if her faith is in You. There is no reason to doubt herself or her journey. For each part is crafted by You, Lord. We pray You lift her head, and reignite that fire in her soul so that she may shine bright for You, just as You intended.

James 1:6
"But when you ask, you must believe and not doubt, because the one who doubts is like a wave of the sea, blown and tossed by the wind."

Amen

Day 121
May 1st

Needing Grace

Tonight, Lord, we pray for the cowgirl that needs Your grace. She pours every ounce of herself into those around her. From her family to her homestead, she gives all she can. But somedays she bends until she breaks. It may come in the form of harsh words, less patience, or just breaking down. Lord, tonight we ask You to give her grace to know that when things get hard, she can lean into You. Blessed are the flexible, for they don't get bent out of shape. Pour Your grace over her and give her the flexibility to breathe when things become too much.

2 Corinthians 12:9
"My grace is sufficient for you, for my power is made perfect in weakness." Therefore, I will boast all the more gladly of my weaknesses, so that the power of Christ may rest upon me."

Amen

Day 122
May 2nd

Season of Waiting

Lord, tonight we pray for the cowgirl waiting. She may be waiting for the right relationship, or for the last mare to foal. She may be waiting for news from the Dr./vet or to hear back about a job. Or she might just be waiting for the days to get a little smoother and the bank account to get a little fuller. No matter the wait Lord, we pray she knows Your hand is in every piece of the puzzle. We pray You give her peace as she waits for answers. Encourage her to remember Your timing is better than her own.

Isaiah 40:31
"But those who wait upon the LORD will renew their strength; they will mount up with wings like eagles; they will run and not grow weary, they will walk and not faint."

Amen

Day 123
May 3rd

Worry

Lord, tonight we pray for the cowgirl that gets in her own way. Sometimes she spends more time worrying when she could just be moving on. She thinks too much and trusts too little. She's her own worst enemy in her own mind. She has a tendency to sabotage things before she even gives them a chance. It may be in her career, her relationships, or just life in general. We pray Lord, for You to speak truth into her life. We pray You bring peace to her worrisome mind. And we pray she seek Your guidance and direction. May she turn over the control she thinks she needs and lay her burdens at Your feet.

Matthew 6:26-27
"Look at the birds of the air: They do not sow or reap or gather into barns—and yet your heavenly Father feeds them. Are you not much more valuable than they? Can any one of you by worrying add a single hour to your life?"

Amen

Day 124
May 4th

Fresh Air

Lord, tonight we pray for the cowgirl that can't seem to catch a break. Maybe it's work, injuries, a toxic relationship, overbearing family, or just the little things that pile up now and then. Whatever the case Lord, she has had all she can take lately and prays for a moment to catch her breath, find her feet, and regain her thoughts. We pray she remembers she can find all of that in You and through You. May You fill her lungs with fresh air full of peace, lift her feet to the solid rock of faith in You on which she can stand, and calm her mind with the promise of better days ahead as You guide her to them. Tough days come and tough days go, but the promise of Your love Lord, is never ending. May she always find comfort in that.

Romans 12:2
"Do not be conformed to this world, but be transformed by the renewal of your mind, that by testing you may discern what is the will of God, what is good and acceptable and perfect."

Amen

Day 125
May 5th

Wings of Refuge

Lord, tonight we pray for the cowgirl that needs a safe place. A safe place to rest her tired mind. A safe place to stand on a firm foundation. A safe place to bring her worries. She has many irons in the fire, Lord. As things get busy and the fire gets hot the risk of getting burned increases and she needs a safe place to set it all down. She has strong shoulders and calluses on her hands, but we pray Lord, she knows she doesn't have to carry it alone. We pray she seeks You for a safe refuge and a place to lay it at your feet. This world throws many things her way to shake her beliefs, but we pray she finds Your word and promises as a firm foundation to stand safely.

Psalm 91:4
"He will cover you with His feathers, and under His wings you will find refuge; His faithfulness will be your shield and protection."

Amen

Day 126
May 6th

Seek God First

Tonight, we pray for the cowgirl that needs to put You first. She needs to seek You first. She needs to put aside her thoughts of what others think or believe. She needs to walk away from the things that no longer serve You (or her). She needs to align her steps in Your direction and not what the world sees. We pray Lord, You help her see the truth in the way You see her. We pray she stops carrying the needless worries that she cannot control and lays them at Your feet. We pray she put aside her selfishness and seek to walk in a way that glorifies You and all You have done for her. Remind her to see blessings not burdens. She prays for conviction and direction Lord, so that she may correct where she has strayed. Give her strength, comfort, and mercy as You guide her steps to put you first in all she does.

Proverbs 3:6
"Seek His will in all you do, and He will make straight your paths."

Amen

Day 127
May 7th

Big Decisions

Lord, tonight we pray for a cowgirl facing big decisions. Life is full of decisions and there is no way around some big ones. But it's hard to know what decisions are the right ones. We pray she leans on You and Your wisdom through the process, Lord. Because in You she will find truth and the answers she seeks. Because You are the way, the truth, and the light. Give her peace in her heart and the truth she is looking for.

Psalm 32:8
"I will instruct you and teach you in the way you should go; I will counsel you with My loving eye on you."

Amen

Day 128
May 8th

Picking Up the Pieces

Lord, tonight we pray for the cowgirl picking up the pieces. It may be mentally or physically. She may be gathering up what is left of her heart and life after a bad break up or other life altering situation. Or she may still be gathering her thoughts and picking up pieces of her livelihood after weeks of storms. No matter the pieces Lord, we pray You hold the fragile pieces together as she gathers them. We pray You hold her together also Lord, as she feels like she may be falling apart too. We pray You bring her strength to take this challenge and see You in it. We pray You bring her the grace and direction to take the pieces and build something greater. For we know Your plans are greater Lord, we need only to keep seeking You to find it.

Jeremiah 29:11
"For I know the plans I have for you," declares the LORD, "plans to prosper you and not to harm you, plans to give you hope and a future."

Amen

Day 129
May 9th

A Sound Mind

Lord, tonight we pray for the cowgirl struggling within her own mind. Whether it's stress, or nerves, or too many emotions, this struggle is one that takes a toll on her. A cowgirl's plate is usually full and when her mind struggles it makes all her other tasks more difficult. We pray Lord, that You strengthen her as she powers through her day. We pray You bring her peace when she feels her nerves start to build. And we pray for comfort when her emotions overwhelm her. May she find strength and peace in Your word.

2 Timothy 1:7
"For God has not given us a spirit of fear, but of power and of love and of a sound mind."

Amen

Day 130
May 10th

Cowboy Partner

Dear Lord, tonight we want to come to you in prayer for the cowboys in our cowgirls' lives. The ones that support their cowgirls in every way. Every wild idea, every stubborn streak, and every dream she chases. A true cowgirl can certainly do it on her own and many certainly do. But tonight, we give thanks to the good-hearted man standing next to her, the one who works hard to help those dreams come true. And stands back when he sees that stubborn streak starting to brew. If there is trouble in the relationship Lord, we pray You help them look in their hearts to find that common ground that brought them together. May You continue to guide and bless this team.

Thessalonians 5:11
"Therefore encourage one another and build each other up."

Amen

Day 131
May 11th

Healing Hands

Lord, we come to you tonight to pray over our cowgirls that need healing. It may be for herself or others. It may be mental, emotional, physical, or a combination of them. Whatever the case Lord, she comes to You broken and at a loss at where to turn next. She cries out in hopes that You hear her to ease the pain. Her faith is big and strong, but as the days drag on her heart gets heavy. We pray Lord, that you lift her weary soul, may she find strength on Your shoulders. We pray You be the soft place for her to land when the day has been too much. We pray You take control over the situation and give her mind rest. We pray for Your healing hand of mercy over her and the situation.

Jeremiah 30:17
"For I will restore you to health And I will heal you of your wounds,' declares the LORD."

Amen

Day 132
May 12th

Stubborn Streak

Tonight, we pray for the cowgirl that is a little too stubborn for her own good. She's not great at asking for help and most of the time she prefers to fix things herself. She has a big heart, but she can be hard to love and finds it hard to let others in. She was built to work hard and push through incredible adversity, but sometimes she needs to remember it's ok to let others lend a hand. We pray she remembers to take pause to let others in and allow for help to be given. We pray for grace on the days that her stubborn streak gets the best of her. And we pray that even though she struggles to let others in, that she always looks to You and seeks Your guidance.

Hebrews 10:24
"And let us consider how we may spur one another on toward love and good deeds"

Amen

Day 133
May 13th

Comfort of God

Lord, tonight we come to You with prayers of comfort for the cowgirl that needs to feel You near. Like a scared child clings to the leg of their parents our cowgirl is clinging to Your word and promise of better days. Whether it's sickness, or injury, or a situation that has broken her spirit we pray Lord, that when she hits her knees, You meet her there to lift her head and fill her heart. Fill her heart with hope and remind her soul of Your word which says, "For I know the plans I have for you," declares the LORD, "plans to prosper you and not to harm you, plans to give you hope and a future."

Jeremiah 29:11.
"We pray she remembers You will never leave her, and whatever she faces she is never alone."

Amen

Day 134
May 14th

"My Grace is Sufficient"

Dear Lord, tonight we pray for the cowgirl who needs grace. She feels buried under the weight of the never ending "to do" list and the constant needs of the livestock and family. Maybe her job is hectic, her schedule is packed and tonight the world just feels heavy. Help her to remember that she can't control the outcome, but she can control her focus on You. She can receive the grace You freely give, and she can choose to offer grace to others. When the days are long and the work feels hard, she needs to remember that the battle is won and your grace Lord, is sufficient.

2 Corinthians 12:9
"But he said to me, '"My grace is sufficient for you, for My power is made perfect in weakness."' Therefore, I will boast all the more gladly about my weaknesses, so that Christ's power may rest on me."

Amen

Day 135
May 15th

"I Will be with you"

Lord, tonight we pray for the cowgirl that is over her head. It may be one big project, a bunch of little ones, or just her every day full plate. No matter the scenario, she feels like she has over promised and can't help but under deliver. She has spread herself too thin and there isn't much left to go around. Her goals are big, and her drive is bigger, but sometimes the obstacles in the way eat away at her confidence to finish. We pray Lord, that she knows when it's ok to say no to adding another thing to her plate. We pray she turns the mental load over to You to give her mind peace that You are in control. And we pray that You give her strength to see through the obstacles and keep pushing through to the finish line. Renew her strength, her faith, and her resilience.

Isaiah 43:2
"When you pass through the waters, I will be with you; and when you pass through the rivers, they will not sweep over you. When you walk through the fire, you will not be burned; the flames will not set you ablaze."

Amen

Day 136
May 16th

Seeking Forgiveness

Lord, tonight we pray for the cowgirl that seeks forgiveness. It may be for herself, or it may be forgiveness that she needs to give. If she seeks the forgiveness for herself Lord, we pray she remembers where the ultimate forgiveness comes from.

Psalms 65:3
"Though we are overwhelmed by our sins, You forgive them all."

If it's forgiveness she needs to give Lord, we pray she looks to You for strength and guidance. Some forgiveness must come without an apology or remorse. These tend to be the hardest wrongs to forgive, but we pray she remembers You are the forgiver of all sins, hers included. We pray she remembers she is called to forgive others as You have forgiven her. May she lean on You and find the strength to give forgiveness and set her mind free.

Amen

Day 137
May 17th

Guidance

Lord, tonight we pray for the cowgirl that is heading towards adventure and goals but wants to stay grounded in You. She is ready to spread her wings and soar towards her dreams head-on. But she also knows the pressures of the outside world could pull her eyes off of You. We pray Lord, that she remembers that she can soar and fly highest when she stays focused on You and Your strength. If she strays from You her heart will get heavy, and the weight of the world will be too much to carry alone. We encourage all her dreams and pray she looks to You for the guidance to see them through. And we pray she remembers You will always be with her no matter where life takes her.

Deuteronomy 31:6
"Be strong and courageous. Do not be afraid or terrified because of them, for the LORD your God goes with you; he will never leave you nor forsake you."

Amen

Day 138
May 18th

Raising Babies

Lord, tonight we pray for the cowgirls raising the next generation in this world full of uncertainty. One day after the next the world seems to throw a new obstacle to navigate. As a mother and caregiver her life's purpose feels like she needs to protect all that comes their way. And some days she feels like there isn't enough of her to go around. We pray Lord, You set her mind at ease knowing Your hand is over all of these uncertain times.

Esther 4:14
"Perhaps you were born for such a time as this."

We pray Lord, she finds comfort in knowing that You have created us all for this specific time. We have been created to be a light in the darkness. May she stand bold and strong and raise her babies to do the same.

Amen

Day 139
May 19th

Questions and Answers

Lord, tonight we pray for the cowgirl struggling for answers. So many times, things happen that we don't understand, and we beg and plead for answers. She knows that those questions and situations don't always come with answers, but still her heart aches to understand. We pray Lord, that You bring Your comfort and unconditional love to cover her soul. We pray You bring her peace that even in the hardest situations she can know You have the best in store. May she hold strong in her faith and keep on the journey ahead.

2 Corinthians 1:3-4
"Blessed be the God and Father of our Lord Jesus Christ, the Father of mercies and God of all comfort, who comforts us in all our affliction, so that we may be able to comfort those who are in any affliction, with the comfort with which we ourselves are comforted by God."

Amen

Day 140
May 20th

Restless Mind

Lord, tonight we pray for the cowgirl whose mind needs a break. She's pretty sure, if turned loose, her thoughts could spin a hole in the ground. She has so much to keep track of in that mind of hers that sometimes she feels like she doesn't have room in there for much else. We look to Your word Lord, and we see:

Matthew 6:25-27
"Therefore I tell you, do not be anxious about your life, what you will eat or what you will drink, nor about your body, what you will put on. Is not life more than food, and the body more than clothing? Look at the birds of the air: they neither sow nor reap nor gather into barns, and yet your heavenly Father feeds them. Are you not of more value than they? And which of you by being anxious can add a single hour to his span of life?"

We pray Lord, she reads this over and over until it soaks in and covers her in comfort. May she turn over her worries and clear her mind.

Amen

Day 141
May 21st

Keep Hustling

Lord, tonight we pray for our cowgirls that are out there hustling everyday just trying to make it work. She might not have the 1D horse, or the fancy truck or trailer. Maybe she can't afford or find a trainer to help. But her dreams are just as valid as the next girl, and her determination maybe even a little more. She works hard and she's thankful for all she does have, and she knows the Lord is guiding her steps. She finds joy in the journey wherever it takes her, and knows life is more than outward appearance. But sometimes the side looks, and whispers steal her joy, and she feels defeated before she steps in the arena. Lord, we pray You lift her head and hold it high. Remind her of Your word,

Ephesians 2:10
"For we are His workmanship, created in Christ Jesus for good works, which God prepared beforehand, that we should walk in them. May she renew her strength and determination in You."

Amen

Day 142
May 22nd

Gift of Grace

Lord, tonight we pray for the cowgirl that needs Your Grace. She knows she isn't worthy of the blessings that surround her. She just prays to give You the glory at the end of the day. She knows that she is saved by Your grace through her faith. She seeks Your grace daily as she struggles to feel worthy. We pray she remembers that Your love is unconditional and freely given. She prays for strength to rise up on days she has fallen. She prays for guidance on days she lacks direction. And she prays for peace when the noise of the world gets too loud. And may she always be reminded of the promise and gift in Your word.

Ephesians 2:8
"For it is by grace you have been saved through faith, and this not from yourselves; it is the gift of God."

Amen

Day 143
May 23rd

Unconditional Love

Lord, tonight we pray for the cowgirl needing Your unconditional love. The love that transcends all limitations this world carries. She seeks a love that sees past her flaws, and beyond her past mistakes. The love of this world can be so fleeting and full of expectations. Sometimes it makes her feel unworthy, and incapable of loving even herself. We pray Lord, You meet her right where she is, just as she is, and show her Your love. Bring into her heart Your unconditional, unfailing Love. The one love that sees past all her flaws and mistakes and gives grace! May she feel the warmth of knowing You love her always, even when she feels unlovable. May she lay her head down tonight with her heart full of Your love.

Romans 8:39
"Neither height nor depth, nor anything else in all creation, will be able to separate us from the love of God that is in Christ Jesus our Lord."

Amen

Day 144
May 24th

Get Your Joy Back

Lord, tonight we pray for the cowgirl that needs to get her joy back. Between current events and the daily struggles she faces, she has felt her joy slipping away. She has felt the hardness of this world slowly creep into her life. We pray Lord, that You remind her of the blessings surrounding her every day. May she take pause and find blessings instead of burdens. We pray You breathe life and love back into her soul. Remind her of Your unconditional love. We pray she seek the joy in every step of her journey even on the hard days. May she take pause and give You thanks.

Romans 15:13
"Now may the God of hope fill you with all joy and peace as you believe in Him, so that you may overflow with hope by the power of the Holy Spirit."

Amen

Day 145
May 25th

Blessings over Burdens

Lord, tonight we pray for the cowgirl that is over her head. She may be over her head at work, at home, with her horse, or just all of it combined. She knows this because she gets overwhelmed and frustrated easily instead of finding a moment to pause and breathe to figure things out. We pray You give her those moments to find pause and seek You. We pray she finds the courage to say no to the things that don't bring her joy and don't serve You. We pray You give her strength to push through on the tough days and may she seek You when she can't do it on her own. We pray she finds blessings instead of burdens in her busy-ness. May she find peace in knowing that she doesn't have to have it all figured out and that she can turn to You for guidance.

1 Timothy 6:12
"Fight the good fight for the true faith. Hold tightly to the eternal life to which God has called you."

Amen

Day 146
May 26th

Choices

Lord, tonight we pray for our cowgirl that is faced with a choice she isn't sure how to make. It may be for herself, her family, or her livestock. This decision could change everything, and she isn't sure if it will be for the better or worse. Regardless of the situation Lord, she wants to make the right one, the one that aligns with Your will. May she not be persuaded by guilt, fear, or greed. For these are all feelings Lord, and they don't come from You. Give her faith to look to You for answers. Find her in the quiet of her mind to make the decision that is best because You know what is best not based on her feelings. Guide her heart Lord, and we know she will follow.

Proverbs 3:5
"Trust in the LORD with all your heart and lean not on your own understanding"

Amen

Day 147
May 27th

Self Care and reflection

Lord, tonight we come to You to pray for our cowgirls who are working on themselves. It may be to be a better wife, mother, sister, daughter, or friend. Or maybe she's looking to be a better competitor, a better rider, or a better trainer. She may need to build on her confidence or find a way to calm her mind in chaos. Whatever character building she is after Lord; we pray she knows You are right beside her cheering her on. We pray she knows her strength to do all these resides in You and through You she can do all things. We pray when things get hard or she struggles, to remember why she started, You remind her to find joy in the journey. And You will see her through to the other side.

Philippians 4:13
"I can do all this through Him who gives me strength."

Amen

Day 148
May 28th

Protection

Lord, tonight we pray for our cowgirls that need Your hand of protection. It may be over her health, her mind, or a situation. She prays You guide her steps to avoid danger along her path. May she turn her thoughts to You when evil tries to invade them. And we pray You step in to intervene in any toxic situation.

Psalm 91:4-5
"He will cover you with his feathers, and under his wings you will find refuge; His faithfulness will be your shield and rampart. You will not fear the terror of night, nor the arrow that flies by day."

We pray Lord that she is reminded that You see all and know the protection she seeks. We pray she seeks You for the solution.

Amen

Day 149
May 29th

Horse Troubles

Lord, tonight we pray for the cowgirl struggling with a horse. It may be a new horse that she is still working out the kinks with. Maybe it's her old faithful that has been lame every time she turns around. Or maybe it's a new problem that isn't quite sure how to navigate. Sometimes the horse world can be a tough place to ask for help, so we pray You surround her with a good support system. We pray her mind and her heart are open to hearing other opinions and ideas even if they are hard to hear. And we pray You guard her heart from those that don't have her best interests in mind. As in any struggle Lord, we pray that she knows You walk beside her and never leave her. May she feel Your guidance and comfort every step of the way. And as this struggle resolves Lord, we pray she remembers to pay it forward and lend a hand the next time around.

Luke 18:27
"But he said, 'What is impossible with men is possible with God.'"

Amen

Day 150
May 30th

Balancing Act

Lord, tonight we pray for our cowgirls that feel like they are in the middle of a balancing act. On one hand they work around the clock making sure needs and ends are met for her family and farm. On the other they pray to work on themselves and help others around them wherever a need arises. From bottle calves to burp cloths, and bookkeeping to bedtime stories their plates are full. And as the plates get overloaded the stress builds. And some days they feel like all the plates they've been balancing come crashing to their feet. We pray Lord, for them to feel Your grace on those days. We pray they know You will help them carry the load, she need only to ask.

Matthew 11:28-30
"Come to Me, all you who are weary and burdened, and I will give you rest. Take My yoke upon you and learn from Me, for I am gentle and humble in heart, and you will find rest for your souls. For My yoke is easy and my burden is light."

Amen

Day 151
May 31st

God's Will

Lord, tonight we pray for the cowgirl seeking to do Your will. Whatever the situation may be, even if it's not what she desires, Lord. She prays for clarity, she prays for guidance, and she prays for peace within the decision. She knows Your plans are better than her own and she prays Your will be done over her life. She knows that it's hard when her will doesn't align with Yours and she prays for comfort if that is the case. Above all she prays to be a light to show Your love no matter the scenario or the outcome. May she rise above disappointment with grace. And may she praise You in every triumph. Give her wisdom Lord, and patience to see Your will be done and strengthen her faith as she walks each step of the journey with You.

Job 23: 10-11
"But He knows the way that I take; when He has tested me, I will come forth as gold. For I have stayed on God's paths; I have followed his ways and not turned aside."

Amen

Day 152
June 1st

Being Busy

Lord, tonight we pray for the cowgirl with a busy week ahead. Summer has been in full swing with a full schedule that has her running circles somedays. Between competitions, kids, horses, cattle, and family she has her hands full. With all the running she's doing it's easy to lose track of time, time for herself and time for You, Lord. We pray she takes a moment tonight as she lays her head down to breathe and look to You. We pray she seeks You in all she does and that You make her paths straight.

Proverbs 3:6
"In all your ways acknowledge Him, and He will make your paths straight."

Give her guidance and strength for the week ahead.

Amen

Day 153
June 2nd

God Hears You

Tonight, Lord, we pray for our Cowgirl that needs to feel heard. The world is so loud and full of noise. Noise from the news, social media, the to-do list on the fridge, and all opinions of family or friends. Sometimes she can turn the noise off outside her head, but it just keeps blaring inside her mind. The 'what ifs', 'should haves', and 'maybe I'll find time tomorrows' keep her mind in a constant battle for peace. She just wants to feel like someone is listening and understands. When we look to Your word we see,

Psalm 10:17
"You, Lord, hear the desire of the afflicted; You encourage them, and You listen to their prayers."

We pray she takes great comfort to know she is heard and You are near. May she carry that blanket of comfort as she lays her head down tonight and may it quiet the noise.

Amen

Day 154
June 3rd

Our Hope is in Him

Tonight, Lord, we pray for the cowgirl that needs to believe in herself again. She needs to remember why she started this crazy wild dream to begin with. She feels like she has pushed so hard towards these dreams that now she feels like she's hanging out on a limb. The doubts in her mind and the rough road have her feeling maybe she should give it up. Tonight, we want to lift her head and fill her heart with the purpose You have given her. Remind her of that purpose and that drive and remind her why she started. We pray Lord, she takes pause to find joy in the journey, and remember not to compare her journey with other's highlight reel. We pray You fill her heart with the drive to believe in what You have given her.

1 Timothy 4:10
"That is why we labor and strive, because we have put our hope in the living God..."

Amen

Day 155
June 4th

God's Hand

Lord, tonight we pray for the cowgirl that needs You to intervene. She needs You to step in and be the Lord of her life and save her from a situation, a decision, or maybe herself. Sometimes life gets ahead of her, and she gets all wrapped up in it. She knows You are the way and the truth and the life and her soul begs and cries out for Your guidance. We pray Lord, that You look down on her with forgiveness and grace. May she feel that wash over her and find comfort. May she remember that no matter how many steps she has taken away from You the return back to You is only one. One step back to You, one door to her heart to open and ask You in. Meet her right where she is Lord, and heal her brokenness. Restore her faith and breath life back into her bones.

Zechariah 1:3
"Return to me,' declares the Lord Almighty, 'and I will return to you,' says the Lord Almighty."

2 Chronicles 30:9
"For the Lord your God is gracious and compassionate. He will not turn his face from you if you return to him."

Amen

Day 156
June 5th

Cowgirl Gypsy

Lord, tonight we want to pray for our cowgirl gypsies. These traveling souls are always on the move, Lord. It may be for work, competition, or just bouncing from one life journey to the next. They love the adventure of it all Lord, but all that travel can be a little tiresome and sometimes she just needs a solid place to plant her feet and rest her head. When those places are few and far between, we pray Lord, that You be her rock to stand on and her soft place to rest her mind. Keep her safe as she chases those white lines and remind her she's never alone no matter where her travels take her.

Psalm 139:9-10
"If I rise on the wings of the dawn, if I settle on the far side of the sea, even there Your hand will guide me."

Amen

Day 157
June 6th

Use Your Gifts

Lord, tonight we pray for the cowgirl that is thankful for the opportunity to dream. She is thankful for the passion that You placed in her heart and the gifts/talents You have given her in order to chase that dream. We pray for her strength and faith on the days that the journey is difficult. We pray for grace and mercy on the days that she falls short. And we pray above all that she gives You all the glory in every success. We pray she seek You for guidance and celebrate the small victories with You as well as the big ones. We pray she uses all of this to shine a light for You, and to be a light for others to see Your love through her.

1 Peter 4:11
"Do you have the gift of speaking? Then speak as though God himself were speaking through you. Do you have the gift of helping others? Do it with all the strength and energy that God supplies. Then everything you do will bring glory to God through Jesus Christ. All glory and power to Him forever and ever!"

Amen

Day 158
June 7th

God's Power

Lord, tonight we want to pray for the cowgirl feeling discouraged. She feels like she takes one step forward and two steps back. She sees the goal ahead and somedays it seems right around the bend, but others she wonders if the fight is worth it. It may be outside factors or her own self confidence getting in her way, but whatever the case she isn't sure if she is strong enough to keep going. This is when we remind her that she doesn't need to be strong enough because her success doesn't depend on her strength alone.

2 Corinthians 12-9
"'My grace is sufficient for you, for My power is made perfect in weakness." Therefore, I will boast all the more gladly about my weaknesses, so that Christ's power may rest on me.'"

We pray Lord, she reads that verse over and over until she feels Your power overcome her doubts.

Amen

Day 159
June 8th

Endurance with Jesus

Lord, tonight we pray for the cowgirl running on fumes. Her tank is empty mentally and physically. She pushes herself each day to be all the things and be all the places. She runs from the moment her feet hit the ground from one task to the next. Some days it's a thankless and mentally draining job, but she knows that there are blessings in the burdens. And she knows that there is joy in journey, but sometimes it's hard to find. We pray for strength Lord, the strength to see past the thankless days and see the precious memories made. We pray for grace and mercy on the days that her patience runs thin. We pray that You fill her tank with Your love and faithfulness. Restore her and comfort her on the days that overwhelm her.

Hebrews 12 1-2
"Let us run with endurance the race God has set before us fixing our eyes on Jesus, the author and perfecter of faith."

Amen

Day 160
June 9th

Full Plate

Lord, tonight we pray for the cowgirl with a full plate. She spends her day bouncing from bills to babies or fixing fence to fixing plates. Many days she's working before the sun comes up and long after it goes down, just to make sure the wheels keep turning. Sometimes it feels like the only time anyone notices is if she misses something on the list. We pray Lord, that You remind her she is never alone and that You see each step she takes and that You walk this journey with her. May she remember that although her plate is full, that it is full of blessings.

Luke 12:48
"To whom much is given, much will be required."

Amen

Day 161
June 10th

"I will give you rest"

Lord, tonight we pray for a cowgirl seeking peace. She may be facing the unknown or walking a difficult path. She may be struggling with making a decision or the consequences of one already made. Whatever the scenario Lord, she is seeking peace in her heart. The roller coaster of emotions have left her heart hurt and unsure of where to land. We pray You bring her comfort and the peace she seeks. May she feel Your peace wash over her as You step in and guide her in Your will. We pray she finds You and Your word as a soft place to land her weary mind. We pray Your hand of mercy and grace cover her troubled heart. May she find rest in You.

Matthew 11:28
"Then Jesus said, 'Come to Me, all of you who are weary and carry heavy burdens, and I will give you rest.'"

Amen

Day 162
June 11th

In God's Eyes

Lord, tonight we pray for the cowgirl that needs to see herself through Your eyes. Not the eyes of critical family or friends or an unappreciative boss. But instead, we pray she sees herself through Your eyes of forgiveness and unconditional love. Your eyes that see her flaws but stands beside her anyway. That knows her sin but forgives her anyway. Sometimes the eyes of this world only see what they want to see and her vision of herself gets tarnished. We pray tonight she looks in the mirror and sees the beauty that you see, and the child of God that stands before her.

1 Samuel 16:7
"For the Lord sees not as man sees: man looks on the outward appearance, but the Lord looks on the heart."

Amen

Day 163
June 12th

Pause and Listen

Lord, tonight we pray for our cowgirl that needs to pause and listen. She's a busy woman with a full plate, but it's important for her take the time to listen to You and Your word. She holds You in her heart but needs to remember to open her mind and pause her busy thoughts to let You in there, too. For in all her busyness she needs to not only hold You in her heart but also to hear and feel Your guidance. We pray Lord, she takes the time as she lays her head on the pillow tonight to just lay in silence and listen for You. And we pray You come to her to fill her heart with all that she needs to hear.

John 10:27-28
"My sheep hear my voice, and I know them, and they follow Me. I give them eternal life, and they will never perish, and no one will snatch them out of My hand."

Amen

Day 164
June 13th

Summer Slump

Lord, tonight we pray for the cowgirl in the summer slump. She's hit the road hard this year. Making up for last year's disappointments and taking advantage of every opportunity. She's had some good wins and no doubt great memories, but she seems to have hit the summer slump. The one that slowly creeps in and just lingers. One tough break after another, mile after mile, and the bank account is seeing more withdrawals than deposits. She's starting to wonder if she should just stay home. We pray Lord, that she remembers this journey she is on, win or learn, is a blessing and one that not everyone gets the opportunity to do. We pray she leans on You when things get tough and remembers to thank You when she catches her next break. Because the summer slump doesn't last forever, and her turn to shine will come again. And we pray that when it does her light shines for You!

Romans 8:28
"And we know that for those who love God all things work together for good, for those who are called according to his purpose."

Amen

Day 165
June 14th

Strength from the Lord

Lord, tonight we pray for the cowgirl needing strength. It may be strength to keep pushing forward, or strength to walk away from a situation. No matter the situation Lord, she knows it is bigger than her and more than she can do on her own. We pray You give her courage to face it head on, we pray You bring her grace when she loses her footing, and we pray You bring her peace when her mind races with the unknown.

Isaiah 41:10
"So do not fear, for I am with you; do not be dismayed, for I am your God. I will strengthen you and help you; I will uphold you with My righteous right hand."

May she stand on the firm foundation of Your word and may it strengthen her soul.

Amen

Day 166
June 15th

Starting Over

Lord, tonight we pray for our cowgirl looking to start over. She's made mistakes, she learned hard lessons, and she wants to do things differently. She's learning to forgive. To forgive others and forgive herself. She smiles and works hard to hide the past she carries, but it's a heavy burden Lord, and she no longer wants to carry it alone. She prays to lay it all at Your feet Lord.

Isaiah 43:18
"Forget the former things; do not dwell on the past."

We pray You heal her heart where it is broken and help her mend relationships. We pray You give her the fresh start and new perspective she seeks.

Amen

Day 167
June 16th

Against the Odds

Lord, tonight we pray for the cowgirl that feels like she's fighting against the odds. She may be working her way from the bottom up. Maybe she is the first in her family to try something. Or maybe she doesn't feel like she has any support from those around her. Whatever the case Lord, we know that as she pursues the passion that You put in her heart, You will be there with her every step of the way. We pray she knows that no matter the obstacles in her way her faith can move mountains. And with You and through You she can do everything.

Philippians 4:13
"I can do all things through Christ who gives me strength."

Amen

Day 168
June 17th

A Patience Lesson

Lord, tonight we pray for the cowgirl learning a lesson in patience. Of all the lessons she's learned Lord, this one feels like it's getting the better of her. She is a worker, a planner, and a goal setter. When things don't go according to her plan or schedule, she struggles to adjust and understand how it fits into Your plan, Lord. We pray You remind her that it is by faith not sight that she is to be guided. We pray she recalls all the things You work out better for Your good, Lord. We pray she seeks Your will and not her own. We pray with these things she finds the patience she needs to travel through this trial Lord. Be with her and guide her, comfort her and bring her peace in Your truth.

2 Corinthians 5:7
"For we walk by faith, not by sight."

Amen

Day 169
June 18th

Old Friends

Lord, tonight we pray for the cowgirl that is thankful for old friends. The ones that saw her grow up through the awkward years. The ones that stood beside her through her toughest times. The ones that have rode shotgun swapping old rodeo stories at 2am. The ones that she can call months apart and still pick up right where she left off. And the ones always willing to lend a shoulder to cry on or a spare room to sleep. The older she gets the more she realizes how much of a blessing these old friendships are. The rare true bond that only old friends carry because they have seen her through every stage of life and grown with her. We pray Lord, that You lay special blessings over these friends. We pray Your hand of protection over them and the friendship and may they share many more years.

Proverbs 27:9
"Sweet friendship refreshes the soul."

Amen.

Day 170
June 19th

Facing Trials

Lord, tonight we look to Your word to guide our prayer for the cowgirl going through trials. She knows this life comes with ups and downs and that no road is without its bumps. But knowing doesn't always mean handling it is easier. We pray she reads this verse and finds the growth that these trials give her. We pray she takes them on with an open mind to find a better cowgirl on the other side. A stronger, more patient, and more dedicated cowgirl with a better relationship with You. We pray You guide her feet to the path for growth and be with her every step.

James 1: 2-3
"Consider it pure joy, my brothers and sisters, whenever you face trials of many kinds, because you know that the testing of your faith produces perseverance."

Amen

Day 171
June 20th

Trouble in Love

Tonight, Lord, we pray for the cowgirl that has had a rough go in the love department. She has maybe kissed her fair share of frogs or hasn't found anyone even worthy of that. She may have just ended a relationship she thought was the real deal, or maybe she's trying to find a way out of one. She is busy with so many other things that finding a partner for all of life's ups and downs would be nice, but that doesn't mean it's easy. We pray Lord, that she remembers that just as You are preparing her for her partner, that You are preparing her partner as well. Your word says,

Proverbs 18:22
"He who finds a wife finds a good thing."

We pray she remembers she is the prize worthy of finding, not the other way around. We pray she focuses on You and her relationship with You. Give her Your peace and unconditional love as she waits for the partner You are preparing for her.

Amen

Day 172
June 21st

Faith Over Fear

Lord, tonight we pray for our cowgirl battling fear. It may be fear of the unknown, fear of the future, or lingering fear from a past hurt. As cowgirls Lord, many times we push past fear and move forward anyway. But that doesn't mean that the fear isn't still there and that it can't still affect our actions. We pray Lord, that You take away that fear by reminding her of Your promises. We pray she remembers that she shouldn't fear the future because she knows who holds the future. We pray she releases her fear of the unknown because You know all, Lord. And we pray Lord, that You lay Your healing hands over her and take away the past hurt. May she lay her head in peace tonight putting her faith over her fear.

Psalm 56:3-4
"When I am afraid, I put my trust in You. In God, whose word I praise, in God I trust; I shall not be afraid."

Amen

Day 173
June 22nd

God's Handiwork

Tonight, Lord, we want to pray for our cowgirl that is following that passion You put in her heart.

Ephesians 2:10
"For we are God's handiwork, created in Christ Jesus to do good works, which God prepared in advance for us to do."

She knows the talents and gifts she has been given from You carry a responsibility. She feels the joy in fulfilling Your plans for her and she strives to be a light for You in the process. Tonight, Lord, we pray she seeks You in all she does. We pray she looks to You to guide her hands and feet. May they be Yours to do Your work. Her talents are Your gift to her, may what she does with them be her gift to You.

Amen

Day 174
June 23rd

Support System

Lord, tonight we pray for the cowgirl support system. The mom's and dad's, grandmas and grandpas, aunts, uncles, brothers, sisters, and friends that have become family. The ones that always answer the phone and show up when You need it. Holding babies or recoding our runs. From riding shotgun at 2am eating gas station snacks to waiting up with you walking a colicky horse. The ones that run the chutes before or after work. The ones that work two jobs to help pay for the things you need. And the ones that tell you what you need to hear even when you don't want to hear it. May we cherish them, and the memories made along the way. We pray blessings and protection over them. We pray they always know the impact they have made.

1 Corinthians 16:14
"Let all that you do be done in love."

Amen

Day 175
June 24th

Accepting Help

Dear Lord, tonight we pray for the cowgirl who needs to ask for help. She takes on what feels like the weight of the whole world on her shoulders. Mostly she is happy to do it, happy to feed the animals, care for the kiddos, maintain the property, fix supper, clean the house, do the laundry and work all day at her job. She sometimes provides a listening ear or shoulder to cry on and is a problem solver for her friends and family. She gives of her time and ability freely, and without a tally of what would be owed to her in return. Lord, help her to remember that she can't pour from an empty cup, she can ask others for the same help she would freely give to them if the roles were reversed. Remind her that we are called to share in each other's burdens, and we walk a hard and narrow road toward You. Send her encouragement through others and through dedicated time spent in Your word. Speak life into her and remind her that she doesn't have to do it all alone!

Galatians 6:2
"Carry each other's burdens, and in this way you will fulfill the law of Christ."

Amen

Day 176
June 25th

Unexpected Goodbye

Lord, today we pray for the cowgirl facing an unexpected goodbye. The kind that pulls the rug right out from under her and shatters her heart beyond recognition... The kind that leaves her breathless and unsure where to turn. But we pray she turns to You, Lord. We pray You gather up those shattered pieces and hold her in Your loving arms. Lord, there is nothing to ease the heartache for her right now, but we just pray You bring her peace in knowing her loved one is with You. We pray she can find some peace to know that their loved one is not in pain, but instead reunited with those that have passed on before. We pray You surround her with love from family and friends to help hold her together as she faces each day ahead.

Matthew 5:4
"Blessed are those who mourn, for they will be comforted."

Amen

Day 177
June 26th

Big Expectations

Lord, tonight we pray for the cowgirl with big plans, big goals, and big expectations for herself. She sees Your blessings and opportunities all around her and works hard to put them to use. But with big plans, goals, and expectations can come big disappointments and big stressors. We pray Lord, she seeks Your guidance and direction. We pray for grace and comfort when her plans don't align with Yours. And we pray she seeks to be a light to show the word Your love through her. May she take the opportunities in front of her and make the most of each one and give You all the glory.

Proverbs 16:3
"Commit to the LORD whatever you do, and he will establish your plans."

Amen

Day 178
June 27th

"God is Within her"

Tonight, we pray for the cowgirl stepping out in faith. She feels the pull You have laid in her heart Lord, to step out into something. Stepping out in faith can be new and exciting, but also scary with the unknown. She has felt the tug on her heart for a while and her feet just kept dragging hoping maybe the tugging would stop. But she knows Your plans for her are great and can only be greater if she takes the leap in faith. We pray Lord, You cover her in comfort and the peace that passes all understanding. We pray she remembers Your promises and Your purpose for her can only be fully revealed if she follows along in faith.

Psalm 46:5
"God is within her, she will not fall."

Amen

Day 179
June 28th

Seasons of Life

Dear Lord, tonight we pray for the cowgirl who is in a season. A season of growth, of change, a season of waiting or maybe a season of pain. Each of these come with different challenges and triumphs. When she can't see the end of this hard season Lord, remind her that You will carry her when she can't take one more step, You will sit with her when she needs to rest and You will make a way for her to see it through to the end. Seasons change, and she will go through so many, but in the midst of them all let her see Your provision and feel Your guidance. Help her focus on the blessings You provide each day and provide her peace that surpasses all understanding.

Lamentations 3:22-24
"Because of the Lord's great love we are not consumed, for His compassions never fail. They are new every morning; great is your faithfulness. I say to myself, 'The Lord is my portion; therefore, I will wait for him.'"

Amen

Day 180
June 29th

Trust in the Lord

Lord, tonight we pray for the cowgirl who needs guidance for a decision. She has come to a crossroad, and she has a choice to make. She has plenty of talk in her ear from all sorts of sources, but she prays for the decision that is right for her and aligns with Your will for her. She prays, Lord, You will open the doors You wish for her to walk through and close those not meant for her. We pray, Lord, she trusts this and gives You control so she may continue her journey, trusting You will guide her steps.

Proverbs 3:5-6
"Trust in the Lord with all your heart and lean not on your own understanding; in all your ways submit to Him, and He will make your paths straight."

Amen

Day 181
June 30th

Season of Waiting

Lord, tonight we pray for our cowgirls in a season of waiting- waiting for plans to line up, waiting to find the right relationship, waiting for a healing, or waiting for it to be her turn. We all have seasons of waiting and some are longer than others. She tries to be patient, Lord, as she knows Your plans for her are better than her own. We pray she takes this season of waiting as an opportunity to grow and ready herself for the plans You have for her. When we look to Your Word, Lord, You are clear in what You ask of us.

Psalm 37:7
"Be still before the LORD and wait patiently for Him. So we pray for patience and guidance as we navigate this season of waiting. May she seek your plans as she prepares to bare much fruit."

Amen

Day 182
July 1st

Walking Away

Tonight Lord, we come to you with prayers for the cowgirl who is walking away from something for the promise of something better. It may be a walking away from a relationship, a job, or a situation. She prays to walk in the path You have for her even if it means she must take a turn to the unknown. She knows that when something no longer serves You and Your plan for her, it is time to walk away, but that doesn't always make walking away easy, Lord. We pray You lay a blanket of comfort over her heart and her mind. May she focus her mind on You and Your promises for a better future. Guide her path and make it straight.

Romans 12:13
"So let us put aside the deeds of darkness and put on the armor of light."

Amen

Day 183
July 2nd

Patience

Lord, tonight we pray for the cowgirl who needs more patience. She needs more patience for her kids, her husband, and her work. She needs more patience for Your plan, her plans, her animals and her projects. Her life feels chaotic, and she just wants a minute to breathe and find your peace. The disorder and disruptions of everyday life seem to send her into a tailspin lately. We pray for a moment to breathe. We pray for her to seek Your guidance because we know You will guide her to the peace and patience she needs. We pray for Your mercy as she navigates her feelings of anxiety and stress. May she feel Your presence and feel the peace that passes all understanding. In that peace, may she find the patience to navigate her day.

Romans 12:12
"Rejoice in hope, be patient in tribulation, be constant in prayer."

Amen

Day 184
July 3rd

Starting Over

Tonight Lord, we come to You to pray for the cowgirl who feels like she is starting over. It may be a career, a horse, a relationship, or a move to somewhere new. Just when things felt like they were on the right track, something pulled the rug out from under her. Now, she must regroup and try again. Although she knows You have a plan for her, Lord, the thought of having to start over can feel overwhelming. We pray, Lord, she remembers the times before when You saw her through. We pray she looks at this as a fresh start, an opportunity for greater things, and a chance to make positive change. Change can be scary, Lord, but we pray she focuses on Your promises and plan for her.

Jeremiah 29:11
"For I know the plans I have for you," declares the LORD, "plans to prosper you and not to harm you, plans to give you hope and a future."

Amen

Day 185
July 4th

For our Military

Lord, tonight we pray for our military cowgirls and their families and friends. We pray thanks over the sacrifices they make everyday that many won't ever know. We pray for the countries and the people they protect. Lord, we pray You are with them and comfort them. We pray Your hand of protection over the families who stand behind the uniforms and hold down the households while their loved ones are away. May they find peace in Your Word that You go with them and stand beside them wherever the road may lead.

Psalm 91: 2,4
"This I declare about the LORD: He alone is my refuge, my place of safety; He is my God, and I trust Him... He will cover you with His feathers. He will shelter you with His wings. His faithful promises are your armor and protection."

Amen

Day 186
July 5th

"For Such a Time as This"

Lord, tonight we pray for the cowgirl who needs restoration. She needs to feel like herself again. Maybe she lost herself having kids or immersed in her work. Maybe she strayed from her relationship with You or family and friends. Whatever the scenario, Lord, we pray You breathe life and love back into her soul. We pray when she looks in the mirror, she sees herself through Your eyes and feels Your love surround her. We pray she remembers the woman she was, embraces the woman she is, and seeks guidance for the woman she is becoming. For as this life changes, so will she, but we pray she remembers You have created her for greatness in every step of her journey. Give her grace on the days she feels like she falls short. And bring her peace and strength on the days that are difficult.

Esther 4:14
"For perhaps you were created for such a time as this."

Amen

Day 187
July 6th

Blanket of Peace

Lord, tonight we pray for the cowgirl who seeks peace. Things in her life are stealing her joy and disrupting her peace. It may be her job, family trouble, or a struggle in her own mind. She feels things spinning out of her control and prays for You to step in and regain peace. She prays You bring the peace that passes all understanding. May she feel the blanket of peace fall over her tonight as she closes her eyes to sleep. May she sleep with confidence that You are in control.

Philippians 4:6
"And the peace that surpasses all understanding will guard your hearts and minds in Christ Jesus."

Amen

Day 188
July 7th

"My Help Comes from the Lord"

Lord, tonight we pray for the cowgirl who is trying to shift her perspective. She's in the middle of a trial that is not an easy walk. But she walks it, knowing You take every step with her along the way. Still, she finds herself feeling frustrated and discouraged. We pray You turn her eyes on the joy that can be found even on her hardest days. We pray You fill her heart with Your unconditional love, even on the days she feels alone and misunderstood. We pray You bring her peace when the tough choices come her way. Guide her eyes, her heart, and her soul to focus on Your good, Lord. Adjust her outlook to see Your goodness in all things.

Psalm 121 1-2
"I lift up my eyes to the mountains— where does my help come from? My help comes from the LORD, the Maker of heaven and earth."

Amen

Day 189
July 8th

Remember

Lord, tonight we pray for the cowgirl who is stressing. It may be a worthwhile worry, or something completely out of her hands. She may be stressing about making the right decision, or worried about what others think. No matter the worry or the stress, Lord, we know that ultimately the control belongs to You. We pray, Lord, she has the faith and the strength to turn over all anxieties to You. We pray she remembers all the past worries that You cast away. We pray she remembers all the moments that when turned over to You, they turned out perfectly. So, we pray she takes pause to release the worries and anxieties and give them to You. Give her peace, Lord.

Mathew 11 28:30
"Come to me, all you who are weary and burdened, and I will give you rest. Take my yoke upon you and learn from me, for I am gentle and humble in heart, and you will find rest for your souls. For my yoke is easy and my burden is light."

Amen

Day 190
July 9th

Slow Down

Lord, tonight we pray for the cowgirl who feels like it's all moving too fast. The days fly by in a blur and then her head hits the pillow in exhaustion. She tries to find joy in the journey, but sometimes she feels like she is just trying to get down the road without the wheels falling off. Everyone tells her, "slow down, life goes too fast". She says, "I know" with a twinge in her voice because she doesn't know how. We pray, Lord, that You bring her comfort as her head hits the pillow tonight. Slow her racing thoughts and show her the joy of her days. Remind her that even on her busiest days, blessings are to be found. We pray she finds a moment for herself to slow down unapologetically, even if only for a moment. May she appreciate the peace as the world flies by around her. Bring her clarity and guidance to navigate the hustle and bustle. May she remember so many of the things she has now are the things she once prayed for.

Matthew 6:33-34
"But seek first the kingdom of God and his righteousness, and all these things will be added to you. Therefore do not be anxious about tomorrow, for tomorrow will be anxious for itself."

Amen

Day 191
July 10th

Her Turn

Lord, tonight we pray for our cowgirl wondering when it's going to be her turn. She knows waiting is a part of the journey, but she's starting to get frustrated. She's worked hard, she's put in the time, the effort, and the money. She sees others' highlight reels and wonders, why not her? Why not today? We pray You give her the patience she needs to get to the next mile marker of her journey. We pray you remind her of where it started and the progress she's made. Open her eyes to the blessing of this opportunity to dream the big dreams and chase the big goals. In You, all things are possible if we align our hearts with You and feed not her own selfish desires, but Your desires for her. Lord give her the wisdom to see the difference, and keep pressing on.

2 Peter 3:9
"The Lord is not slow to fulfill his promise as some count slowness, but is patient toward you"

Amen

Day 192
July 11th

Tested Faith

Lord, tonight we pray for the cowgirl who feels her faith tested. She feels this world and things around her pushing her in ways she didn't see coming. The rollercoaster of emotions seems more than she can endure, and she wonders how much more she can take. We pray for perseverance, Lord. We pray for comfort and guidance as she continues down this journey seeking You and joy, even in the difficult steps. Your Word in

James 1: 3-4
"For you know that when your faith is tested, your endurance has a chance to grow. Let perseverance finish its work so that you may be mature and complete, not lacking anything."

We pray she reads this and finds comfort in Your plan for her to persevere and grow. We pray she finds growth and peace through this test of faith. May she draw near to You now and find peace.

Amen

Day 193
July 12th

Silent Battles

Lord, tonight we pray for the cowgirl fighting a silent battle. The one she doesn't speak of, the one only you and she know about. It may be an illness that shows no outward appearance or anxiety that she manages to smile through. Maybe it's an addiction that she hides too well, or a toxic relationship hidden behind a Facebook highlight reel.

No matter the battle, Lord, we pray she seeks You for comfort and guidance. We pray You guide her and give her the confidence and courage to seek the help she needs. For although she may feel it, she isn't alone in this battle. We pray she knows You are always with her and will never leave her side.

Exodus 14:14
"The Lord will fight for you; you need only to be still."

Amen

Day 194
July 13th

Feeling Lost

Lord, tonight we want to lift up the cowgirl who is feeling lost. She's found herself on a path that she isn't so sure of anymore. She prays for guidance, peace, grace, and forgiveness. It may have been one wrong turn or several, but no matter, the return is just one step. We pray Lord she remembers that You said,

"I will stand at the door and knock..."
Revelation 3:20

We pray she opens the door to her heart and lets You in. We pray she finds her way in You and she finds the peace and grace she has been seeking. May she always remember the Lord said,

"I have loved you with an everlasting love."
Jeremiah 31:3

Amen

Day 195
July 14th

Conflict

Lord, tonight we pray for the cowgirl in the middle of conflict. It may be with family or a friend, someone at work, or maybe she's found herself in the middle of someone else's conflict. Conflict is never easy and sometimes the hardest part is looking in the mirror to see what can be fixed. She knows, Lord, she is only capable of changing herself. If change is needed on the other side, we pray she seeks You to intervene. She prays for resolution, peace, and forgiveness on both sides. She prays for guidance to be the woman of God You call her to be. To act on compassion and forgiveness instead of simply reacting to pain. We pray You be with her Lord see her through these troubled waters. Steady her ship and guide her between the waves.

John 14:27
"Peace I leave with you; my peace I give to you. Not as the world gives do I give to you. Let not your hearts be troubled, neither let them be afraid."

Amen

Day 196
July 15th

Head and Heart

Lord, tonight we pray for the cowgirl struggling between her head and her heart. Her heart wants to believe the best in all things and stays hopeful even in the toughest of times. Her head can't help but see and hear the evil in the world. Current events have her questioning the motives of everything around her. She clings to Your Word for that is the only place she finds truth. We pray, Lord, for You to guide her heart and her mind and fill them with truth and love. We pray for her mind to be opened to the love still found in those around her. And we pray for protection over her precious heart.

Proverbs 4:23
"Above all else, guard your heart, for everything you do flows from it."

Amen

Day 197
July 16th

Clarity in the Chaos

Lord, tonight we pray for the cowgirl who feels like there isn't enough of her to go around. From bills to pay and babies to feed. From horses to ride and events to plan. She's fixing problems while trying not to step into another one. She wears many hats, but there is still only one of her. She spends her day pouring into everyone around her only to find her cup empty at the end of the day. We pray for peace, Lord. We pray for clarity in the chaos. We pray You pour Your unconditional love into her and wrap her in Your comfort. Give her strength and remind her the days are long, but the years are short. The only thing that stays the same is that everything changes. Remind her that even on the days she feels empty and tired, that You still stand beside her, thankful for her servant's heart. Bless that heart, Lord, overfill it with Your love. Fill her with joy and peace.

2 Corinthians 4:6
"For God, who commanded the light to shine out of darkness, hath shined in our hearts, to give the light of the knowledge of the glory of God in the face of Jesus Christ."

Amen

Day 198
July 17th

Heart Horse

Lord, tonight we pray for our cowgirl's heart horse. The one who made them the rider they are today. The one who pushed them to the next level, maybe with a buck or two. The one who gave them soft hands and tolerated them as they were learning. The one who met them in the pasture after school and let them cry into their mane after a bad day. They knew all her secrets and never judged. Maybe she still has that horse; maybe they are buried under a tree out back. But tonight, Lord, we pray thanks over these gifts from You. The One who made them, and the One who saved them. And we pray for all the cowgirls out there still seeking their heart horse.

James 1:17
"Every good gift and every perfect gift is from above, coming down from the Father"

Amen

Day 199
July 18th

God Prepares

Lord, tonight we come to you with the cowgirl who needs to know she is enough. She is enough to accomplish her goals. She is enough on the days she doesn't finish the list of to-dos. She is enough even when the world says otherwise. Because in You and through You she draws strength; she draws power, and she gains the will to be all You have called her to be. Somedays that calling feels like too much, and she thinks she isn't the right one to be called. But the truth is, she is the right one and she is enough. Because God doesn't make those decisions based her self-worth, He bases them on what He has instilled in her and prepared her for. We pray, Lord, lift her up, blow wind in those sails, and send her on the journey of greatness You have prepared just for her.

Psalm 138:8
"The Lord will fulfill his purpose for me; your steadfast love, O Lord, endures forever. Do not forsake the work of your hands."

Amen

Day 200
July 19th

Faith in the Struggle

Lord, tonight we pray for the cowgirl who needs to see the bigger picture. She needs to find joy in her journey. She needs to find blessings in her burdens. She needs to find harmony within the hard. She knows Your plans are better, but sometimes her patience runs thin in the valleys of this journey. Her frustrations wear on her faith, and she wonders if her struggles are truly a part of her journey, or if she's taken a wrong turn somewhere. We pray, Lord, that You remind her that just because it's hard doesn't mean it's not a blessing. We pray she seek Your guidance and stay the course. May she feel Your peace and comfort even on the difficult days. We pray You meet her right where she is and remind her of Your promises. Restore her faith and give her the patience to persevere.

Deuteronomy 31:6
"So be strong and courageous! Do not be afraid and do not panic before them. For the LORD your God will personally go ahead of you. He will neither fail you nor abandon you."

Amen

Day 201
July 20th

Spirit of Hope

Tonight, Lord we pray for the cowgirl who needs to trust. She needs to trust in Your Word and promises. She needs to trust in Your plan. And she needs to trust and believe in herself. She needs to trust her strength, her heart and the passion You put in her heart. This world can be cruel and the lies it spreads can make doubt creep in. We pray, Lord, for Your truth to fill her soul. We pray for the courage to step out and trust her feet to move forward. We pray You bring light and truth to any darkness and doubts that come her way. May she feel Your truth surround her and may she trust in the journey ahead.

Romans 15:13
"I pray that God, the source of hope, will fill you completely with joy and peace as you trust in him. Then you will overflow with confident hope through the power of the Holy Spirit."

Amen

Day 202
July 21st

Healing and Strength

Tonight Lord, we come to You for the cowgirl needing healing and strength. The healing may be for her, for a friend or family, for an animal, or maybe a troubled relationship. No matter the scenario, Lord, we know You see her struggle and hear her cries. We pray, Lord, that she leans on You when things get tough, and we pray she seeks You for direction when she feels lost. May You bring her strength and grace to see her through. Lord, we pray she bring healing and comfort for all those involved. May she find strength in You to persevere.

Isaiah 41:10
"So do not fear, for I am with you; do not be dismayed, for I am Your God. I will strengthen you and help you; I will uphold you with my righteous right hand."

Amen

Day 203
July 22nd

Battle Has Been Won

Lord, we come to you tonight for the cowgirl who needs to remember the battle is already won. This world can be tough, and she finds herself trying to be tougher. She finds herself pushing back on all that is pushing her and ends up feeling exhausted. We pray, Lord, she remembers this world is only temporary and You have already paid the ultimate price for our eternity. We pray that on the days she is at her wits end, tired and frustrated, she can find rest and comfort in You and Your Word. We pray for grace and mercy on the days her patience runs thin.

2 Chronicles 20:17
"You need not fight this battle. Take up your positions, stand firm, and see the salvation of the LORD on your behalf."

Amen

Day 204
July 23rd

Strength from the Lord

Lord, tonight we pray for the cowgirl who needs to catch a break. She works hard each day, one foot in front of the other just waiting for things to turn around. She has been in a season of struggle, Lord, and she prays for a break in her battle. She prays for a glimpse of the light at the end of this struggle. We pray, Lord, You give her some rest from the worries in her mind. We pray she remembers that no matter the struggle, You walk with her every step. We pray she remembers no matter the battle, You will fight for her. Bring her strength to persevere, cover her in comfort, and give her peace that passes all understanding.

2 Timothy 4:17
"The Lord stood by me and gave me strength so that through me the message might be fully proclaimed."

Amen

Day 205
July 23rd

You Are Enough

Lord, tonight we pray for the cowgirl who's too hard on herself. She puts every ounce of herself into everything she does and yet many days she still feels like it's not enough. From running the household to running the ranch, to balancing babies and checkbooks, her hands are full. She's thankful for all the blessings but wonders if she's doing enough. When she spends the day at home doing fun things with the kiddos, she lays in bed at night wondering about all the chores she should have done. And likewise, on the days she spends all day tending cattle or riding horses, the mom guilt hits her hard. We pray, Lord, she knows You recognize and see all she puts in. We pray she knows she is always enough in Your eyes. Fill her heart and soul with love, recognition, and peace.

John 16:33
"I have said these things to you, that in Me you may have peace. In the world you will have tribulation. But take heart; I have overcome the world."

Amen

Day 206
July 25th

God's Plan

Lord, tonight we pray for the cowgirl who's struggling. She's unsure if her struggles mean she should go a different direction or if it's a test of her faith to keep pushing forward. She has faith and trusts to walk through the door of opportunities that You provide, Lord. She knows You will see her through every hill and every valley. But she wonders, Lord, if maybe she has taken a wrong turn somewhere and gone off course. Maybe she has put her plan ahead of Yours and perhaps she needs to do some adjusting. We pray, Lord, that You give her clarity. We pray she seeks You, Your truth, and Your guidance. We pray she remembers You are in control, and we pray she let You be the leader of her life. If she has strayed, we pray You bring her peace as she gets back on course. And we pray You bring her strength and comfort in this part of her journey. We pray she remembers You are the same God on the mountain as You are in the valley, may she seek You always.

Micah 7:7
"But as for me, I will look to the Lord; I will wait for the God of my salvation; my God will hear me."

Amen

Day 207
July 26th

The Lord will Fight

Tonight Lord, we come to You to pray for the cowgirl who needs to open her eyes and her heart to see You move in her life. She needs to let go and stop trying to control everything around her. When she is so focused on trying to get things done and make things happen, she loses the opportunity to sit back and watch You work in her life. As a cowgirl, she may spend days fighting fence that needs fixing, an uncooperative heifer with a fresh calf, or old equipment on a cold morning. But when we look to Your word, Lord, we see

Exodus 14:14
"The LORD will fight for you; you need only to be still."

We remind her, Lord, that even though many days will require the strong will and stubborn work ethic you gave her, some days will require her to pause look to You and be still. For not every fight is hers to take on, may she take a deep breath and seek You for strength and answers.

Amen

Day 208
July 27th

Empty

Tonight Lord, we pray for the cowgirl who is running on E. Her tank runs on empty, and the road looks long and uphill. Whether it's kids or cattle, bills or bottles her hands are full and her ambition is gone. Her patience has run thin and by the end of the day, it hits empty as well. We pray for rest, Lord. The kind that refills her soul and wakes her with new hope and faith. May she cast her worries to You and find peace in Your plan. Give her grace when the patience runs out, and mercy when the day has been too much. May she seek You and find rest in You and Your Word. We pray she find a quiet moment to close her eyes and turn it over to You.

Exodus 33:14
"And the LORD answered, "My Presence will go with you, and I will give you rest."

Amen

Day 209
July 28th

Picking up the Pieces

Lord, tonight we pray for the cowgirl trying to put the pieces together. Maybe she's picking up the scattered bits after one of life's curveballs. Maybe she's trying to arrange all the pieces just to get them into the same place so she can focus. Perhaps she's still working to find that missing piece or figure out why the last one won't fit just right. Whatever the situation, Lord, we know that Your hand is at work in each one. We pray for patience, perseverance, and strength when she feels like giving up. We pray she remembers that no puzzle of life is complete without You at its center. We pray she seeks You for any of the pieces that seem out of place.

Romans 12:12
"Rejoice in hope, be patient in tribulation, be constant in prayer."

Amen

Day 210
July 29th

Restless

Lord, tonight we pray for the cowgirl who is feeling restless. She longs to chase the dreams she sees others chasing. She longs for a relationship, a family or a career. She has a passion in her heart but doesn't see a road to get there. Sometimes she wonders if she took a wrong turn somewhere and finds her mind scrambling to seek ways to get back on track. We pray, Lord, for peace, the peace that only You can provide. We pray she seek You and You give her clarity and direction for the journey ahead. We pray she seek a closer relationship with You, Lord. And we pray she finds the answers she seeks within that relationship. May she be Your hands and feet and step into Your will where her heart and soul will be ultimately fulfilled.

Psalm 138:8
"The LORD will fulfill His purpose for me; Your steadfast love, O LORD, endures forever. Do not forsake the work of Your hands."
Psalm 139:1
"O LORD, You have examined my heart and know everything about me."

Amen

Day 211
July 30th

Finding Quiet

Lord, tonight we pray for our cowgirl who needs quiet. In the world that makes so much noise, she seeks a simple quiet moment to herself with You. From the news and social media to the kids and animals, her ears are filled all day long. Some of the noise that fills her ears is good, but some is full of trouble; ultimately, she just prays for peace. We pray, Lord, You quiet the noise. We pray You still the air around her. We pray she takes if even a moment to hear and feel the quiet You create within her. We pray she feels the peace that passes all understanding even as the world spins chaos around her.

Psalm 119:114
"You're my place of quiet retreat; I wait for Your Word to renew me."

Amen

Day 212
July 31st

Ready

Lord, tonight we pray for the cowgirl who is ready to take on whatever You have in store for her. She is ready to face it head-on even if she doesn't know the road ahead. She knows it won't always be an easy road to travel. But we pray she learns to find joy in the journey. We pray she looks for the message in the mess. Just as she knows there will be challenges along the way, she knows she can find strength and guidance through You. May she move forward with an open heart and open mind and step out into faith for this walk with You, Lord. We pray she shine like a beacon of light to show all Your goodness.

Hebrews 13:21
"May He equip you with all you need for doing His will. May He produce in you, through the power of Jesus Christ, every good thing that is pleasing to Him. All glory to Him forever and ever!"

Amen

Day 213
August 1st

Finding Strength

Lord, tonight we pray for the cowgirl who is finding strength she didn't know she had. She's faced situations and circumstances that have tried her heart, her patience, and her faith. Well-meaning people have told her that You won't give her more than she can handle, Lord. However, she knows this isn't true. The trials that push beyond our human limits are meant for us to turn to You, Lord. Your strength is made perfect in our weakness, Lord. We pray she leans on You and feels Your strength. We pray You lift her and carry her through the days that she cannot bare to face. We pray that little by little she find her own strength renewed in Your faithful unwavering love.

Psalm 46:1
"God is our refuge and strength, always ready to help in times of trouble."

Amen

Day 214
August 2nd

House that Build Me

Lord, tonight we pray for the cowgirl's house that built her. The one that shaped her, and molded her into the strong, fiercely independent God loving woman she is today. The days were long and sometimes the nights were longer. Waiting for livestock to bring new life in the spring was full of joy, some heartache, and many sleepless nights. She learned values they can't teach anywhere else. It wasn't easy and it wasn't always fun; what she learned was a great gift. We pray thanks for the families raising the next generation of cowgirls may they be strong; may they be loyal, and may they give You all the glory. We also pray for the cowgirls shaped by a harder journey growing up. We pray they find the path they walked full of life lessons that serve them well today.

Colossians 2:7
"Let your roots grow down into Him, and let your lives be built on Him. Then your faith will grow strong in the truth you were taught, and you will overflow with thankfulness."

Amen

Day 215
August 3rd

Lay it at your Feet

Lord, tonight we pray for the cowgirl who needs to breathe and seek You. Her mind races with the constant hustle and bustle of her day-to-day errands to run, decisions to make, and problems to fix. It seems, everyone and everything need something from her. We pray, Lord, before the weight gets too much to hold, she turns it over to You. We pray she seeks your guidance to make the pieces fit according to Your will. We pray she remembers You are in control and that she can lay it all at Your feet.

Jeremiah 29:11
"For I know the plans I have for You, declares the Lord, plans to prosper you and not to harm you, plans to give you a hope and a future."

Amen

Day 216
August 4th

Riding Solo

Lord, tonight we pray for the cowgirls riding solo. It may be by choice, by circumstance, or just temporary. Either way, she's carrying a heavy load on those shoulders. She might have littles to care for along with holding down the home front. She works so hard to keep a brave face for them. You have given her broad shoulders to carry that load, but tonight, Lord, we pray You lift her heavy yoke and carry it for her. Let her mind rest in You and know that no matter the circumstance she is never truly alone when she carries You in her heart.

John 16:32
"Yet I am not alone, for the Father is with me."

Amen

Day 217
August 5th

Gift of Peace

Lord, tonight we pray for the cowgirl who has choices to make. Choices she isn't sure she wants to make, but knows she needs to. They may be choices she knows will ultimately be for the best, but they still mean big changes. Big choices and big changes are not always easy. We pray, Lord, that she seek Your guidance for Your will to be done. We pray she lay her decisions at Your feet and has faith in Your plan. We pray You bring her peace for the changes that will come.

John 14:27
"I am leaving you with a gift—peace of mind and heart. And the peace I give is a gift the world cannot give. So don't be troubled or afraid."

Amen

Day 218
August 6th

Trust Fall

Tonight Lord, we pray for the cowgirl who has hit a rough patch. Maybe it's lameness, illness, or she's just off her competitive game. The talent is there; the drive is there. She's put in all the work, but she just seems to come short of the success she seeks. We pray she takes a step back to remember where she came from and all the success she's had to get to where she is right now. The path she walks isn't easy and it isn't for everyone, but it is a path she walks with You, Lord. On that walk, she needs to remember You have her best in mind and You won't lead her astray. For the plan You have is greater and even if she doesn't understand the valley she's in, she can trust You will lead her to the other side.

John 13:7
"Jesus answered him, "What I am doing you do not understand now, but afterward you will understand."

Amen

Day 219
August 7th

Perspective

Lord, tonight we pray for the cowgirl who needs a little perspective. Sometimes she finds herself overwhelmed, discouraged, and stressed. She burns the candle at both ends and wonders if the grass is greener on the other side of the fence. We pray she takes a step back, Lord, to see the bigger picture. We pray she see the blessings in her "burdens" and remembers that others pray for the "problems" she has. We pray she realize the grass is greener where you water it. We pray she remembers this life is a journey, and no one said it's a smooth one. We pray she remembers each breath she takes is a gift someone else didn't get to take. May she breathe deep and may You fill her soul with Your grace, mercy and strength. Breathe life, love, and purpose back into her heart.

Corinthians 4:18
"So we fix our eyes not on what is seen, but on what is unseen. For what is seen is temporary, but what is unseen is eternal."

Amen

Day 220
August 8th

Goodbye

Lord, tonight we pray for the cowgirl preparing to say goodbye to her four-legged companion. It may be goodbye after a long life of great memories, or maybe an unexpected goodbye that cuts those memories short. As a rule, goodbyes don't generally come easy, but this one seems particularly hard. She will cherish the memories made and hold them close. We pray, Lord, You comfort her and guide her as she navigates this part of her journey. We pray You bring her strength and grace to help dry her eyes when the tears come. Bring her peace to know she can lay this hurt at Your feet and You will carry it for her and never leave her.

Isaiah 54:10
"For the mountains may depart and the hills be removed, but my steadfast love shall not depart from you, and my covenant of peace shall not be removed," says the Lord, who has compassion on you."

Amen

Day 221
August 9th

Strong Mind

Lord, tonight we pray for our cowgirl's fears. The ones that creep in when our minds get still or our prayer life gets tired. Sometimes the fears are silly and sometimes they feel very real. They may range from work, to family, to the future and everything in between. We pray, Lord, that she remembers You are in control.

2 Timothy 1:7
"For God hath not given us the spirit of fear; but of power, and of love, and of a sound mind."

We pray this reminds her that those fears no matter how real are not from You, Lord, and they hold no power over her. Instead, may she find strength and comfort in Your gifts of power, love, and a sound mind. We pray these things overcome her fear and she stands strong in You and Your Word.

Amen

Day 222
August 10th

Peace that passes all Understanding

Lord, tonight we pray for the cowgirl who needs Your peace. The peace that passes all understanding and only You can provide. Her heart is heavy, her mind is busy, and her plate is full. She feels blessed but stressed and she just needs to lay it at Your feet, Lord. As she lays her head on her pillow tonight, we pray her worries melt away and her mind quiets, not because the things disappear, but because she knows You are in control and You have her covered.

Philippians 4:6
"And the peace that surpasses all understanding will guard your hearts and minds in Christ Jesus."

Amen

Day 223
August 11th

One Step

Tonight Lord, we pray for the cowgirl taking that first step to a better life for herself. It may be a first step away from a relationship that is no longer healthy. It may be a first step toward a healthier lifestyle. Maybe it's away from an addiction or toward a new opportunity. Whatever the step, Lord, we pray she knows You are right beside her. The first step can be the hardest, but we pray she knows each step after is on a path toward a better tomorrow. Whether that first step is bold or shaky, we pray she takes it in faith knowing You hold her future in your hands.

Psalm 119:133
"Direct my footsteps according to Your word; let no sin rule over me."

Amen

Day 224
August 12th

Be Strong in the Lord

Lord, tonight we pray for the cowgirl with a tough week ahead. It may be full of projects and business to handle or tough details and situations. Lord, her heart is heavy, her mind is tired, but she stands firmly on her faith. Her faith is all she leans on as she looks toward the days ahead. May You be the solid rock she stands on, and may Your Word be the soft place she can land. We pray You be her armor, be her refuge, and send her Your strength to see her through. She is steadfast and strong, You are within her; she will not fail. Cover her in Your grace, comfort, and love.

Ephesians 6: 10-11
"Finally, be strong in the Lord and in the strength of His might. Put on the full armor of God, so that you will be able to stand firm against troubles."

Amen

Day 225
August 13th

Cowgirl Comrades

Lord, tonight we pray for our cowgirl tribes. We pray thanks for the girls who jump in the truck with us and drive for miles chasing dreams and white lines. We pray blessings over the ones who hold our babies in one hand and record our runs in the other. We pray peace over the ones who drop all their own troubles to lend a hand in our time of need. The ones who rally around us when we need it most. The ones we don't see for months and then pick right up where we left off. These cowgirls and their friendships are a gift from You, and we are forever thankful.

Proverbs 27:17
*"Iron sharpens iron,
and one man sharpens another."*

Amen

Day 226
August 14th

Partnerships

Lord, tonight we pray for the cowgirl's other half. The ones with whom they share life, raise a family, and run a business. Life with a cowgirl isn't always easy. She can be stubborn and short to temper, but she is loyal to a fault and will love with everything she's got. We pray thanks for the man that stands beside her, encourages her, and loves her even in unlovable moments. We pray You guide him to lead the family as You have called him and to seek You in all he does. For the cowgirl still waiting for her cowboy, Lord, we pray she remembers all good things happen in your time. We pray she seek You first and allow You to prepare her for the partner You have for her. Above all, we pray that they make You the center of all these relationships.

Ecclesiastes 4:12
"For a cord of strands is not easily broken."

Amen

Day 227
August 15th

Straightened Paths

Tonight Lord, we pray for the cowgirl who is ready to take the next step, but is unsure what that step is. Maybe it's a step toward a new relationship, maybe a step out into a new job or career. Maybe she is stepping toward a stronger relationship with You. Whatever the step, Lord, we pray she seeks You for guidance. We pray she takes the time to listen for Your answers before jumping in with both feet. We pray You open the doors that need opening and close the ones that need closing. May she focus on Your will and not her own.

Proverbs 3:5-6
"Trust in the Lord with all your heart, and do not lean on your own understanding. In all your ways seek His will, and He will make your paths straight."

Amen

Day 228
August 16th

Triumph Through Trials

Tonight Lord, we pray for the cowgirl who is thankful for the trials that turned into triumph and the burdens that turned into blessings. So many times in this life, she has found herself on her knees asking, "Why me Lord?" Only to see later Your greater plan unfold before her. Although she doesn't always see the message through the mess, she has grown to understand to trust Your plan. We pray Lord, when the chaos comes, You calm her soul and breathe Your truth into her spirit. We pray she remembers the times she has seen Your greater plan and that she is reminded to keep her faith strong. For Your Word says,

James 1:12
"Blessed is the man who remains steadfast under trial, for when he has stood the test he will receive the crown of life, which God has promised to those who love Him."

Amen

Day 229
August 17th

The Road Less Traveled

Lord, tonight we pray for the cowgirl who needs to let go of the "what ifs". What if I don't make it, what if I fail, what if I made the wrong choice, what if I'm not good enough, what if I mess up, what if people think…? This life is full of opportunities and decisions. At the end of the day, she knows no one is to blame for her fear of the "what if". The truth is the talents given to us by You, Lord, are given with choices, chances, and opportunities. But if we never pursue the passion in our hearts, and we never step out into faith, we may never experience the blessings You have in store. We pray she remembers that even if her "what if" comes true that her Lord and Savior will be right beside her through it all. We pray she remembers that trials happen on the road to triumph, and the road isn't traveled by standing still. May she take the first step and face all of her "what ifs" head on.

Romans 8:30-31
"And those He predestined, He also called; those He called, He also justified; those He justified, He also glorified. What, then, shall we say in response to these things? If God is for us, who can be against us?"

Amen

Day 230
August 18th

Rescue

Lord, tonight we pray for the cowgirl who needs rescuing. It may be a situation she finds herself in, where she doesn't see a way out. Maybe it's her own mind that she needs saving from. No matter the case, Lord, we pray You speak truth into her soul. We pray she trust Your guidance and direction. We pray You bring her the strength she needs to break free from the lies that have tied her back. Remind her that one step at a time is still moving in the right direction. Breathe life and love back into her heart.

Psalm 34:17
"The LORD hears His people when they call to Him for help. He rescues them from their troubles."

Amen

Day 231
August 19th

Growing Roots

Lord, tonight we pray for the cowgirl who wants to take the next step in her walk with You. She wants and needs to step out of her comfort zone and grow in her walk with You. Whether it is growing in her prayer life, stepping out in faith, or working to be a brighter light for You. No matter where she is in her journey, Lord, we pray she remembers every step towards You is a step toward a better tomorrow. May she be strong and brave in her pursuit of a greater relationship with You. We pray You fill her with Your Holy Spirit for direction and may she feel Your unconditional love surround her in every step she takes.

Colossians 2:7
"Let your roots grow down into Him, and let your lives be built on Him. Then your faith will grow strong in the truth you were taught, and you will overflow with thankfulness."

Amen

Day 232
August 20th

Soar on Wings

Lord, tonight we pray for the cowgirl who's giving it all she's got. She's laying it all on the line for a chance at what she's always dreamed of. It may be for her family, for her career, or for her goals in the arena. No matter the scenario, Lord, all her chips are in, and she's leaving nothing left on the table. It's meant long hours, compromise, and sacrifices, but at the end of the day, no matter the outcome, she knows she gave all she had. If the outcome isn't in her favor, Lord, we pray You bring her comfort, and guide her steps moving forward. It may mean more struggles more sacrifices and more compromise, but we pray You remind her she will never be alone in her journey. If success is in her horizon, we pray, Lord, she looks to You and gives You all the glory, because none of it would be possible without Your guidance and direction. No matter the outcome, we pray she continues to pursue the passion that You've put in her heart and find joy in the journey and never give up. We pray she seeks You in all she does and sends the glory Your way.

Isaiah 40:31
"Those who hope in the LORD will renew their strength. They will soar on wings like eagles; they will run and not grow weary, they will walk and not be faint."

Amen

Day 233
August 21st

Hard Summer

Lord, tonight we pray for the cowgirl who's had a hard summer. It's not what she planned, Lord. The goals and shows she watched pass by, the horse that's still unsound, or the training that just didn't quite cut it. She was sure this was it; she was sure it was her turn this time. But somehow another summer is coming to a close, and she feels like so many doors went unopened. As we look to Your Word, Lord, we see

2 Chronicles 15:7
"But as for you, be strong and do not give up, for your work will be rewarded."

We pray, Lord, she reads those words and rises up from her defeated talk. We pray You breathe life back into that passion and purpose You put in her heart. Fill her soul with the fire and desire to live for You and shine a light for You.

Amen

Day 234
August 22nd

Believe in the Journey

Lord, tonight we come to You to pray for the cowgirl who needs to believe again. She needs to believe in herself. She needs to believe in her journey. She needs to believe she can make it through her struggles. Sometimes in the middle of a struggle, her mind turns on itself. She loses her focus on you, Lord, and she loses the vision You put in her heart. We pray, Lord, for you to restore her passion. Renew the vision and remind her of the gifts You have given her. We pray, Lord, that You fill her heart with Your unconditional love. May she feel Your presence and guidance. May she begin to believe again.

Romans 15:13
"Pray that God, the source of hope, will fill you completely with joy and peace because you trust in Him. Then you will overflow with confident hope through the power of the Holy Spirit."

Amen

Day 235
August 23rd

"I Will Hear"

Tonight Lord, we pray for the cowgirl who needs to know You're listening. She needs to know You hear her and feel peace in her heart. This world is so full of noise, it feels hard to get a word in. So many people giving unsolicited opinions and judgement, she just wants to talk to the One who matters. We look to Your Word for answers, Lord, and we see that in

Isaiah 65:24
"Even before they call, I will answer, and while they are still speaking, I will hear."

We pray as she reads this, she remembers that You are always listening. We pray she finds comfort in knowing You hear the words spoken from her heart or her lips. As she lays her head to sleep tonight, may You grant her peace that passes all understanding for a restful sleep.

Amen

Day 236
August 24th

Love One Another

Lord, tonight we pray for the cowgirl thankful for the cowgirl tribe that has surrounded her from the very beginning. The ones who went with her to look at that first horse, the ones who camped in the back of the trailer without living quarters at weekend shows, and the ones who always answered the phone when she needed help. She's thankful for the tribe that has cheered, videotaped, and sat shotgun through every up and down in her journey. We pray thanks for the blessings of each of them and we pray for protection and blessings to them in return.

Romans 12:10
"Love one another deeply as brothers and sisters. Take the delight in honoring one another."

Amen

Day 237
August 25th

Discouraged

Lord, tonight we pray for the cowgirl feeling discouraged. She feels hurt and a little let down. She feels like the evil in this world is stealing her joy and it has left her discouraged. We pray, Lord, for You to go to battle for her. We pray You fight the fight she knows she cannot win alone.

Psalm 23:4
"Even though I walk through the darkest valley, I will fear no evil, for You are with me; Your rod and Your staff, they comfort me."

We pray she feels the comfort of Your presence over her troubles. We pray she feels encouraged knowing You are fighting for her.

Amen

Day 238
August 26th

Breathe

Lord, tonight we pray for the cowgirl who needs to breathe. Between the chaos of her day and the mental and emotional strain, sometimes she feels like she is suffocating. Sometimes she feels like she spends her day rushing from one thing to the next and she forgets to just stop and breathe and appreciate the blessings that surround her. We pray You breathe life and love back into her lungs. May she remember the purpose You put in her heart and the joy that it brings. We pray she remembers joy and it brings a breath of fresh air to her tired mind. We pray that even on the toughest days, she look to You and remember she only has to take it one breath at a time, one step at a time, one foot in front of the other.

Job 33:4
"The Spirit of God has made me, and the breath of the Almighty gives me life."

Amen

Day 239
August 27th

Settle the Mind

Tonight Lord, we pray for the cowgirl who has a nervous mind. Sometimes from the moment her eyes open, she feels the anxiousness start to build within her. She prays to give it up to You, but sometimes her mind keeps hitting the reset button and she's back to her worries for the day. It may be worries about work, family or the future. Whatever the worries, Lord, she prays for Your peace. The lasting peace that only You can provide. Lord, she wants her heart and mind to settle. We pray she lay it all at Your feet and put her restless mind at ease. Tonight, we ask for sweet restorative sleep so that she can face the day ahead without a nervous heart.

John 14:27
"Peace I leave with you; My peace I give to you. Not as the world gives do I give to you. Let not your hearts be troubled, neither let them be afraid."

Amen.

Day 240
August 28

Trusting the Plan

Lord, tonight we pray for the cowgirl trusting in Your plan. She knows in her heart it's better than she can plan on her own. Lord, you have proved over and over when You come through it's in a big way. Bigger and better than anything she would have asked for or done on her own. Yet she finds her mind racing; her plans turning in her head. Because even though Your timing is best, the waiting is still so hard. Lord, she prays for peace and forgiveness when she tries to take over instead of trusting. Tonight, we pray You fill her heart with the peace that passes all understanding and that she may find rest in trusting Your plan.

Philippians 1:6
"I am sure of this, that He who started a good work in You will carry it on to completion until the day of Christ Jesus."

Amen

Day 241
August 29th

Calm

Lord, tonight we pray for the cowgirl seeking calm in her chaos. It may be work, home, family, livestock, or even the weather. She finds herself feeling defeated and short on answers. She doesn't like feeling out of control and unsure of the future. We pray You bring peace to her chaos. Cover her in Your love and grace. May she feel Your mercy surround her. We pray You guide her through the days she feels lost and may she find comfort in giving You control. Most of all, we pray she hears Your Word, and it speaks to her soul.

Jeremiah 29:11
"For I know the plans I have for you," declares the LORD, "plans to prosper you and not to harm you, plans to give you hope and a future."

Amen

Day 242
August 30th

Comfort in Loss

Tonight, we pray for the cowgirl struggling with loss. It may be a friend or family but the hurt cuts like a knife. It may be a month, a year, or a decade ago but she still feels the burn in her throat and the ache in her heart like it was yesterday. They say that time heals, but the truth is that time just makes it easier to hide. She gets better at putting the pain away in the little box in her mind. Sometimes the memories overtake her with smiles, sometimes tears. We pray she finds more smiles than tears tonight, and that she can find rest in the good memories. May she find comfort in knowing they are with You now, and you never truly lose someone when you know where they went.

Psalm 73:26
"My flesh and my heart may fail, but God is the strength of my heart and my portion forever."

Amen

Day 243
August 31st

God IS Love

Lord, tonight we pray for the cowgirl who needs to feel your unconditional love. She may have lost a loved one or hasn't found the one for her. She may be going through a rough season in her relationship, or maybe ended a relationship that wasn't right. No matter the situation, Lord, her heart aches to love and be loved in return. She knows You have plans for her, bigger than her own understanding. On the hard days, we pray You bring her peace and mercy. We pray You cover her heart and soul in Your love, Your unconditional love.

1 John 4:16
"So we have come to know and to believe the love that God has for us. God is love, and whoever abides in love abides in God, and God abides in them."

Amen

Day 244
September 1st

Unexpected

Lord, tonight we pray for the cowgirl working through the unexpected. There are no promises on this earth, only the truth in Your Word to guide her. Within her journey, she has learned to navigate better the highs and lows and find the joy. But the unexpected still throws her curveballs, Lord. We pray she remembers You are always in control, and nothing is unexpected to You. We pray that when she feels out of control that she remembers to lay it all in Your hands.

Jeremiah 17: 7-8
"But blessed is the one who trusts in the LORD, whose confidence is in Him. They will be like a tree planted by the water that sends out its roots by the stream. It does not fear when heat comes; its leaves are always green. It has no worries in a year of drought and never fails to bear fruit."

Amen

Day 245
September 2nd

Finding Rest

Tonight Lord, we pray for the cowgirl who is burning the candle at both ends. She feels like if she stopped moving, she would run right into herself. She stays busy, constantly working through the ups and downs. Even when the tough days come her way, she puts her head down and stays focused on the goals ahead. She is thankful for the opportunities in front of her and the struggles that have made her stronger. But some days, she just needs a soft place to land; some days she needs a place to rest her weary mind. We pray, Lord, she finds rest in you. We pray she finds peace in the work she puts in to do Your will. We pray she finds comfort in Your word and finds rest in the mercy and grace in Your unconditional love. Even on days that feel like too much, we pray she remembers all the moments You saw her to the other side, and that this too will come to pass with You by her side.

Exodus 33:14
"My Presence will go with you, and I will give you rest."

Amen

Day 246
September 3rd

Lay it Down

Tonight Lord, we pray for the cowgirl who lays it all at your feet- the stress, the worry, the sickness, the injury, the wins, the losses, the victories, and the disappointments. She claims none of it; it belongs to You. Her strength fails her, but Your strength prevails. Her worry drowns her, but Your truth surpasses all. Even in her success, the victory rests with You. Where she needs healing, we pray You bring complete restoration. Where she needs peace, we pray You bring the peace that passes all understanding. We pray for her mind and soul as she navigates difficult and challenging seas, Lord. But she will not fear for she knows her Savior walks on water.

Isaiah 44:22
"I have swept away your offenses like a cloud, your sins like the morning mist. Return to Me, for I have redeemed you."

Amen

Day 247
September 4th

Weakness

Lord, tonight we pray for the cowgirl who is struggling with a weakness. It may be physical or mental. It may be noticeable to others, or something she keeps to herself. Maybe it's something she's been working her whole life to overcome, or maybe it's something new she's learning to work through. No matter the weakness, Lord, we pray she remembers that she is still fearfully and wonderfully made by You. We pray she seeks and finds strength in You. When we look to Your Word, we find the strength in answers.

2 Corinthians 12: 9-10
"But he said to me, 'My grace is sufficient for you, for my power is made perfect in weakness.' Therefore, I will boast all the more gladly about my weaknesses, so that Christ's power may rest on me. That is why, for Christ's sake, I delight in weaknesses, in insults, in hardships, in persecutions, in difficulties. For when I am weak, then I am strong."

May these words bring her strength to keep pushing through and shine Your light.

Amen

Day 248
September 5th

God's Handiwork

Tonight Lord, we pray for those cowgirls seeking purpose through their passion. She prays for the way to turn the passion You have put into her heart into a purpose for Your glory. Some days she wonders if she's spinning her wheels chasing her own selfish desires, or if she is following Your calling for her, Lord. We pray You give her courage and guidance for Your plan for her. As we look to Your Word we read

Ephesians 2:10
"For we are God's handiwork, created in Christ Jesus to do good works, which God prepared in advance for us to do."

This reminds us that God indeed has a purpose for us and he has already prepared us for it. Reassure her, Lord, that she is already prepared, she just needs to look to You for her guidance.

Amen

Day 249
September 6th

Chosen

Lord, tonight we pray for the cowgirl trying to follow Your lead, shine Your light, and be the woman You have called her to be. We pray she seeks You for opportunities and is brave enough to walk through the doors You open. We pray You show mercy on the days she doesn't understand the road You ask her to walk. We pray others see You and Your love when they look at her. We pray You show her guidance and grace when the road she walks gets difficult. As a cowgirl, Lord, she spends a lot of time out in the beautiful world You created, may she find You in every moment of her day. Guiding her, loving her, and protecting her along the way.

Romans 8:30
"And having chosen them, He called them to come to Him. And having called them, He gave them right standing with Himself. And having given them right standing, He gave them His glory."

Amen

Day 250
September 7th

Stuck

Lord, tonight we pray for the cowgirl who feels stuck. Stuck in a relationship, a job, or maybe stuck in her own thoughts. She knows the journey here on earth isn't promised to be easy. However, she finds herself feeling like she has missed the turn that drives her out of the situation she's in. She can't help but feel like she's stuck on a continuous loop of bad news and disappointments. We pray for clarity, Lord. We pray for guidance and direction. We pray for grace on the days she falls short of her goals and expectations. We pray for strength to break the cycle that has her feeling stuck. May she feel You near and trust Your Word even on the days that are difficult to travel.

2 Corinthians 4:16-18
"Therefore we do not lose heart. Though outwardly we are wasting away, yet inwardly we are being renewed day by day. For our light and momentary troubles are achieving for us an eternal glory that far outweighs them all. So we fix our eyes not on what is seen, but on what is unseen, since what is seen is temporary, but what is unseen is eternal."

Amen

Day 251
September 8th

Hurting

Lord, tonight we pray for the cowgirl who is hurting. Her heart hurts over the way things are going in the world, over a family situation, or over something or someone who hurt her. She finds herself trying to put on a brave face to get through the days because she knows the "show must go on" in a cowgirl's busy world. She is brave, and tough, and strong and knows how to push through the hardest of trials. However, sometimes she just needs a soft place to fall when it all hits too hard. She needs a solid rock to stand on when the waters rise higher. We pray, Lord, You cover her in a blanket of grace and peace she can safely fall into. And we pray she stands tall on Your Word as a solid rock for her faith.

Psalm 34:18
"The Lord is near to the brokenhearted and saves the crushed in spirit."

Amen

Day 252
September 9th

Letting Go

Lord, tonight we pray for the cowgirl who needs to let go, release, or walk away from someone or something. Maybe it's a toxic relationship or situation. Perhaps it's something that is no longer helping her grow. It may be an apology she knows in her heart she will never get, or maybe it's forgiveness that she's withheld. Whatever the situation, Lord, we pray she remembers it's ok to take a step back or move away from something or someone that is not healthy. We pray You open her eyes and her mind if there is something keeping her from seeing the truth, Lord. We pray You bring her strength and guidance on the journey ahead.

Philippians 3 13-14
"Forgetting what is behind and straining toward what is ahead, I press on toward the goal to win the prize for which God has called me."

Amen

Day 253
September 10th

Uneasy

Tonight Lord, we pray for the cowgirl who feels like she is walking on eggshells. It may be work, family, or a relationship. Whatever the case, she feels unsure of taking the next step for fear of making the wrong one. Every scenario has its own troubles to navigate, Lord, and we pray You help her with each one. But what we pray for most, Lord, is that You bring her peace to remember You are in control and to turn over her anxieties to You. We pray You fill her with the peace that passes all understanding and that she can take her next steps firmly rooted in Your promises. Turn her cautious steps into steps of confidence. Pick her chin up and fill her heart, Lord. May she go boldly with You in her heart.

Isaiah 41:10
"So do not fear, for I am with you; do not be dismayed, for I am your God. I will strengthen you and help you; I will uphold you with My righteous right hand."

Amen

Day 254
September 11th

Against the Grain

Lord, tonight we pray for our cowgirls going against the grain. You build these ladies tough, Lord, because You know the battles they will face. Maybe she's the first in her family to take on this lifestyle, or maybe she has new plans for the family business. She faces opposition no matter which way she turns, and she knows others don't agree. She feels the stares and hears the whispers. But at the end of the day, we pray she knows to whom she belongs. We pray she remembers she is a daughter of the King. We pray that as she goes against the grain, that You have her back to keep pressing forward. For only You know what her tomorrow holds, Lord, and only You can prepare her. May she seek You and find that strength.

2 Samuel 22:33
"It is God who arms me with strength and keeps my way secure."

Amen

Day 255
September 12th

God Is With Her

Lord, tonight we pray for the cowgirl who is just trying to figure out how to make it to the next day. Each day seems to bring more challenges, and one problem runs into the next. She's tired of feeling like the weight of the world rests on her shoulders. We pray, Lord, You remind her she can lay her burdens at Your feet. We pray she remembers You will carry it for her and she need not walk this valley alone for You are with her even in her darkest steps. We pray she lean on You when her feet get tired, and feel You lift her when her knees give out. Lord, we pray You remind her that this journey is not meant to be traveled alone; that her burdens are not mean to be carried alone. And that if the weight is too heavy it means she is meant to turn it over to You. Lord, we know You will not give her more than she can handle because she isn't meant to handle it alone; she can do all things with You and through You.

Genesis 28:15
"I am with you and will watch over you wherever you go. I will not leave you until I have done what I have promised you."

Amen

Day 256
September 13th

Encouragement

Lord, tonight we pray for the cowgirls who need a little encouragement. Disappointments and setbacks surrounded her this year. Sometimes it feels like the only answer she gets is "no, not this time." She sees the social media highlight reels of others and wonders when it will be her turn. But we pray, Lord, you remind her that a highlight reel is just that, highlights of a life that likely has just as many hills and valleys as her own. We pray she remembers to seek You in those moments of doubt. We pray she remembers all good things come in Your timing, not hers.

James 1:12
"Blessed is the one who perseveres under trial because, having stood the test, that person will receive the crown of life that the Lord has promised to those who love Him."

May she read Your Word tonight and find comfort and encouragement in Your promise.

Amen

Day 257
September 14th

Fighting

Tonight Lord, we pray for the cowgirl fighting. It may be emotional or physical. She may be fighting for herself or others. It may be a something others know about, or a battle she fights in silence. No matter the circumstances, Lord, we know days of fighting leave her exhausted. She longs for peace, mentally and physically. She needs Your grace for the war that rages in her mind daily. As we look to scripture we see

Exodus 14:14
"The LORD will fight for you; you need only to be still."

We pray, Lord, she knows You are in control and You will fight her battles. She need only to trust in You and be still. We pray she seeks You for the hard days and we pray You bring her peace to see her through.

Amen

Day 258
September 15th

Broken Hearts

Tonight Lord, we pray for the cowgirl having to say goodbye. It may be goodbye to a family member or a friend. Maybe it's goodbye to a four-legged companion. Perhaps it's a different kind of goodbye, like leaving a job or old home. These goodbyes come with change, some more than others. And when the goodbye brings pain and sadness, it makes the journey even more difficult. We pray, Lord, that You find her in her pain and darkness and bring her comfort and light. May she feel Your presence and find peace. We pray she seeks You for direction and guidance as she navigates life beyond the goodbye. We pray You shine a light on her journey ahead.

Psalm 34:18
"The LORD is close to the brokenhearted and saves those who are crushed in spirit."

Amen

Day 259
September 16th

Getting it Done

Lord, tonight we pray for our cowgirls who are out there just getting it done. The one who burns the candle at both ends. Most days she doesn't have time to wait around for help, so she is in the thick of it learning and growing as she goes. The one learned by doing because sometimes she has no choice. We pray that she knows You see her Lord. We pray You meet her right where she is and bring her strength and comfort. We pray that on the days she feels like throwing her hands up at it all, that You quietly show her just one more step to keep moving. May she find Your strength and grace and joy in each day.

Isaiah 40:31
"But those who hope in the Lord will renew their strength. They will soar on wings like eagles; they will run and not grow weary; they will walk and not be faint."

Amen

Day 260
September 17th

Courage

Lord, tonight we pray for the cowgirl needing courage. It may be courage to try something new and unfamiliar. It may be courage to leave something unhealthy that is no longer good for her. It may be courage to face something she's put off for too long. Whatever the situation, Lord, we pray she seek You. We pray she feel Your answer in her heart to the difficult questions, and we pray You be her guide when things get tough.

Deuteronomy 31:6
"Be strong and courageous. Do not be afraid or terrified because of them, for the Lord your God goes with you; he will never leave you nor forsake you." Lord be her guide, be her strength and give her peace to know You are with her."

Amen

Day 261
September 18th

Light Shines Through Broken Glass

Lord, tonight we pray for the cowgirl who is thankful for her brokenness. She has hit rough patches, hit rock bottom and climbed her way back up clinging to her faith. Along the way, she's gotten a little banged up and has a few cracks here and there. But when she looks in the mirror, she smiles at the brokenness. She closes her eyes and is grateful for every step of the journey. Because it was in her falls that she felt You picked her up; it was in her deepest hurt that she felt You near; in every broken piece, she sees You. We pray Your light shine through the brokenness. May she always remember that You love each piece of her and the journey that she travels.

2 Corinthians 12:9
"My grace is sufficient for you, for My power is perfected in weakness." Therefore, I will boast all the more gladly in my weaknesses, so that the power of Christ may rest on me."

Amen

Day 262
September 19th

Making a Way

Tonight Lord, we come to You for the cowgirl with too much on her plate. She has so many irons in the fire her flame can't keep up. From her day job to her livestock and everything in-between, there is barely enough time to think. She works hard and will help anyone who needs it, but sometimes she comes up short on time and energy. We pray, Lord, that she takes some time to align her priorities. May she seek Your will and allow You to make a way where there seems to be no way. We pray You clear the clutter in her mind and her day. We pray You bring clarity into her chaos and show her ways to manage change. May she seek You and fill her heart instead of her plate.

Isaiah 42:16
"I will lead the blind by ways they have not known, along unfamiliar paths I will guide them; I will turn the darkness into light before them and make the rough places smooth. These are the things I will do; I will not forsake them."

Amen

Day 263
September 20th

God's Timing

Lord tonight we pray for the cowgirl waiting. She may be waiting for the right relationship, or for the long anticipated harvest. She may be waiting for news from the doctor or vet, or to hear about a job. She might just be waiting for the days to get a little smoother and the bank account to get a little fuller. No matter the wait, Lord, we pray she knows Your hand is in every moment. We pray You give her peace as she waits for answers. And we pray You give her strength and grace as the answers come her way. Encourage her to remember Your timing is better than her own.

Isaiah 40:31
"But those who hope in the LORD will renew their strength. They will soar on wings like eagles; they will run and not grow weary; they will walk and not be faint."

Amen

Day 264
September 21st

Clear Her Mind

Lord, tonight we pray for the cowgirl who needs to clear her mind. She needs to let go of the things that clog up her thoughts- the thoughts that aren't productive, the negative thoughts, and the ones that feed off lies. Instead, Lord, we pray she feed the positive thoughts that restore her faith. We pray she focus on the thoughts that bring her closer to pursuing her passion and the purpose You hold for her. With a clear mind, Lord, she has the opportunity to see what blessings you have for her. May she open her mind to be cleared of clutter and to soak up all of the joy a faith-filled life with You can bring.

2 Timothy 1:7
"For God hath not given us the spirit of fear, but of power, and of love and of a sound mind."

Amen

Day 265
September 22nd

Give Thanks Always

Lord, tonight we pray for the cowgirl whose summer went by too fast. She made a lot of memories, spent too much money, stayed up too late, and ate too much gas station food. Some goals were met, and others were left on the table. We pray thanks, Lord, for the opportunities and the safe travels. We pray she continues to seek You for guidance. We pray she uses the opportunities You give her to bring glory to You. Give her grace when she falls short and give her peace when her mind won't.

1 Thessalonians 5:17-19
"Pray continually, give thanks in all circumstances; for this is God's will for you in Christ Jesus."

Amen

Day 266
September 23rd

Young Cowgirl

Tonight, we pray for our young cowgirls. The ones feeling left out being the "horse girl". She goes to school and goes through the motions just watching the clock until she can head to the barn or next rodeo. This is where she feels at home, where she is surrounded by other horse crazy girls just like her. They share her drive and passion for their equine friends and the sport they play. The kids at school say it isn't a sport, but she spends more time working on her horse and herself each day than most of them will ever spend at practice. So, Lord, instead of feeling left out, I pray she feels empowered. Empowered to know all those women she looks up to now were once the crazy horse girl themselves. Give peace to her little heart and let her know it she's in good company, and it gets better!

Luke 2:40
"The Child continued to grow and become strong, increasing in wisdom; and the grace of God was upon Him."

Amen

Day 267
September 24th

Confidence

Tonight Lord, we pray for the cowgirl stepping out in faith. She is taking that leap, or tip toe, out into something she knows she cannot do alone. Whatever she is facing, Lord, she will need Your help. She will need Your strength when hers fails her; she will need Your guidance when she loses her way, and she will need Your grace when things don't go her way. We pray she finds courage in the steps she is about to take. May she do so with confidence with a heart full of faith that can move mountains.

Isaiah 41:10
"Don't be afraid, for I am with you. Don't be discouraged, for I am your God. I will strengthen you and help you. I will hold you up with My victorious right hand."

Amen

Day 268
September 25th

Family Roots

Lord, tonight we come to you to pray for our cowgirl's family. The family working beside her and supporting her on the rough days when they all lean on each other. The cowgirl family unit can be so strong nothing can waiver the loyalty, but sometimes it can also be tough. Some days tempers flare and opinions vary from person to person. So, we remind our cowgirl that tough times don't last, but tough people do; the future they build together will far surpass and the rocky roads that lay ahead. May You be the roots in which they are grounded.

Colossians 2:7
"Let your roots grow down into Him, and let your lives be built on Him. Then your faith will grow strong in the truth you were taught, and you will overflow with thankfulness."

Amen

Day 269
September 26th

God's Masterpiece

Tonight Lord, we pray for the cowgirl who is different. She may be different from all of the other kids at school because of her lifestyle. Maybe she's different from those at work because instead of "grabbing a drink" after work, she is grabbing a tractor to put out round bales. Maybe she doesn't have the fastest horse; maybe she is older and got a late start to her dream. Maybe she didn't grow up with family who knew all the ropes to teach her. And although some may try to make her believe it, Lord, we pray she remembers different does NOT equal less-than. We pray she remembers she is fearfully and wonderfully made to be exactly who You have called her to be. We pray You give her the strength and the courage to be authentically herself. We pray she never dims her light, the light that shines for You. Fill her with Your unconditional love and peace.

Ephesians 2:10
"For we are God's masterpiece. He has created us anew in Christ Jesus, so we can do the good things he planned for us long ago."

Amen

Day 270
September 27th

What are you trying to Prove

Lord, tonight we pray for the cowgirl looking to prove something, maybe to herself or someone else. Prove she's different, better, or stronger than she or anyone else thinks. Prove she can make it and she deserves it. But we pray, Lord, she remembers she doesn't have anything to prove in Your eyes. We pray she remembers that You have equipped her with all she needs to accomplish all she wants. We pray she seeks Your guidance as she pursues her passion. The passion You have placed in her heart and equipped her for. We pray she takes strength in knowing that You already provided the ultimate proof with Your sacrifice on the cross.

Galatians 1:10
"Am I now trying to win the approval of human beings, or of God? Or am I trying to please people? If I were still trying to please people, I would not be a servant of Christ."

Amen

Day 271
September 28th

God is with You

Lord, tonight we come to you to pray for the cowgirl who feels alone. She may feel this physically or emotionally. It may be by choice or by circumstance. She's strong, Lord, and she can carry a big load on those strong shoulders You gave her, but sometimes the loneliness steals her joy. We pray, Lord, that You lift her chin and remind her that You carry her through all circumstances. Remind her You will never leave her or forsake her.

Zephaniah 3:17
"The LORD your God is with you, the Mighty Warrior who saves. He will take great delight in you; in His love He will no longer rebuke you, but will rejoice over you with singing."

We pray, Lord, You renew her strength and fill her soul with Your presence. May she feel whole again and prepared for anything.

Amen

Day 272
September 29th

Fallen

Lord, tonight we pray for the cowgirl who has fallen. Maybe she has fallen off the path she was on with You. Maybe she's fallen for the lies of the enemy. Perhaps she's fallen into a state of grief and she cannot see her way out. Whatever the situation, Lord, we pray You first bring her comfort and remind her she is not alone. We pray she feel Your grace cover her and her wounds. Bind her up, lift her spirit and renew her faith in You and herself. We pray she leans on You for all her needs, and we pray You restore her.

Psalm 147:3
"He heals the brokenhearted and binds up their wounds."

Amen

Day 273
September 30th

On the Go

Lord, tonight we pray for the cowgirl whose mind won't let her rest. It runs circles around her and considering she is always "on the go" that is a pretty busy noggin. She's a do-er and her mind tries to stay one step ahead. As much as she appreciates her mind's abilities, she also needs a rest. She needs to find a space just to find quiet and a moment to focus. She prays for the time and ability to clear the clutter and just breathe. We pray You bring her peace and grace. May she find the quiet You create Lord and pause in it. We pray she takes the moment to find the clarity she needs. Give her strength to keep moving forward and guidance to stay on course.

Isaiah 26:3
"You will keep in perfect peace those whose minds are steadfast, because they trust in You."

Amen

Day 274
October 1st

Unanswered Prayers

Lord, tonight we pray for the cowgirl who has unanswered prayers. She knows You hear her prayers and she desperately seeks Your answers. We pray, Lord, she remembers that You do indeed hear her prayers and that the answer will come in Your timing not hers. Some prayers require time for the Lord to prepare her to receive the blessing she has coming. For the prayers that receive a "no", Lord, we pray you bring her comfort and remind her that a "no" answer gives way for a greater "yes", and a better blessing than she had prayed for originally. May she find comfort in Your plans, Lord, and find patience in the waiting.

Romans 12:12
"Rejoice in our confident hope. Be patient in trouble and keep on praying."

Amen

Day 275
October 2nd

Let you light Shine

Lord, tonight we pray for the cowgirl who is spread too thin. She has a servant's heart and can't help but give until there is nothing left. She would rather be uncomfortable herself than to see anyone go without help. It fills her soul to give back and give to others, but sometimes she needs to remember to take care of herself too. As the holiday season approaches, Lord, we pray she takes time to enjoy the moments. We pray, Lord, that she remembers that quality beats quantity, and it's ok to let others lend a hand too. We pray You give her rest and refill her heart, Lord. Lift her up and fill her with the blessings that she is to so many others. We pray she takes rest in You and turn things over to Your hands.

Mathew 5:16
"Let your light shine before others, that they may see and glorify your Father in heaven."

Amen

Day 276
October 3rd

Valleys

Lord, tonight we pray for our cowgirls in a valley. Some days she thinks she sees the other side and is on the way back up. Then other days, it seems like a dark hallway that doesn't end. At the end of the day, she knows You are in control and she knows You hold her future in Your hands. Lord, we pray she remembers You know each step she takes before she gets there because You have walked it before her. We pray it brings her comfort to know the valley and darkness are not faced alone, and You are with her every step. We pray You bring her peace and comfort as she takes on another day. We pray she remembers each day is a step toward a better tomorrow. We pray she remembers the God that brings her to the mountain top is the same God that walks with her in the valley.

2 Corinthians 1:3-4
"Blessed be the God and Father of our Lord Jesus Christ, the Father of mercies and God of all comfort, who comforts us in all our affliction, so that we may be able to comfort those who are in any affliction, with the comfort with which we ourselves are comforted by God."

Amen

Day 277
October 4th

Transcendence into Peace

Lord, tonight we pray for the cowgirl who needs to let go of something. It may be the past, or how she thought her future would look. It may be frustration and anger or worries and stress. Whatever the situation, and whatever she is holding on to, it is holding her back. Holding her back from seeing the joy that is possible. Holding her back from finding new love or happiness. Holding her back from the greater opportunities You have in store for her. We pray, Lord, she hands it over to You. We pray she lay the worries, anger, past, and stress at Your feet. We pray she feels the relief as she does so to turn and walk toward the life You have planned for her.

Philippians 4:6-7
"Do not be anxious about anything, but in every situation, by prayer and petition, with thanksgiving, present your requests to God. And the peace of God, which transcends all understanding, will guard your hearts and your minds in Christ Jesus."

Amen

Day 278
October 5th

Quiet Cries

Lord, tonight we need You to hear the quiet cries of the cowgirl's heart. She has a weight she carries, and she needs You to make a way where she sees no way. Lord, she needs You to step in and show her the answer, provide the solution. It may be with her horse, her family, her job, or finances. She may not speak of these worries out loud, Lord, but you see and you know her heart. We pray you move the mountain she sees ahead and provide the way to ease her heart.

Isaiah 43:19
"He will make a way where there seems to be no way."

Amen

Day 279
October 6th

Defeated

Lord, tonight we pray for the cowgirl who is just defeated. Mentally and emotionally. She prays and seeks Your strength, Lord, because hers has failed her. This world can be cruel and no one said it would be fair. Physically, she just keeps pushing through on to the next task and past the mental block. We pray, Lord, that You show her where her mind can rest. Restore her spirit in Your word. Lift her soul and refill her faith. We pray she finds peace in You to rest her mind and recharge.

Mathew 11:28-29
*"Come to me, all you who are weary and burdened, and I will give you rest.
Take My yoke upon you. Let Me teach you, because I am humble and gentle at heart, and you will find rest for your souls."*

Amen

Day 280
October 7th

He will Provide

Tonight, we pray for the cowgirl needing a way out. Maybe it's from a job, a relationship, or another situation. She may not know how to get out, or she may see the way, but it seems too difficult. We pray she looks to You to guide her steps, to show her the way to freedom from whatever binds her. Remind her that she doesn't need to be strong enough, but that her strength resides in You and through You. We pray You open the doors and clear the path, hold her hand and guide her to the other side.

1 Corinthians 10:13
"He will also provide a way out so that you can endure it."

Amen

Day 281
October 8th

First Step

Tonight, Lord we want to pray for the cowgirls who may have strayed. Maybe they used to have a great relationship with You and too much of the world's harshness has gotten in the way. She just isn't who she used to be, Lord, and it hurts her and those around her. Maybe she's reading this or she knows someone who should. Either way, we pray it finds her tonight. May she look around at the life she's living and find that the emptiness she feels is the missing relationship with you, Lord. We pray that she look Your way again, if only for a moment, to realize You have, in fact, never left. You are simply waiting for her to walk Your way again, and tonight we pray she takes that first step.

Isaiah 53:6
"All of us, like sheep, have strayed away. We have left God's paths to follow our own. Yet the LORD laid on him the sins of us all."

Amen

Day 282
October 9th

God's Grace

Lord, we come to you tonight to pray for the cowgirl who needs to feel Your grace. She needs to feel Your forgiveness and unconditional love. The push and pull of the day sometimes runs her patience short. She feels herself fall short of the woman You have called her to be. So we pray, Lord, that that You meet her where she is, whether it's elbow deep in barn chores or rocking the babies to sleep. We pray she feel your presence and peace. We pray she take a step back to see that Your unconditional love covers her in all she does. May she feel Your love and peace and feel Your forgiveness and grace.

John 14:18
"I will not leave you comfortless: I will come to you."

Amen

Day 283
October 10th

Cry Out

Lord, tonight we take pause to pray for cowgirls who feel lost. Maybe she used to feel so close to You but for some reason now, when she prays, You feel so far away. Maybe she feels You near but doesn't know how to make her relationship stronger, to grow in her faith, and to release her worries and stress to You. Whatever the cause, Lord, we pray she remembers no matter how far she strays or how long she turns away, You will always be right there. You are always waiting just one step away. There is nothing she could do to make You turn and leave. You will never give up on her despite what the world tells her. We pray, Lord, when she closes her eyes tonight, she feels Your comfort and power. We pray she releases those worries to You and You give her the peace that passes all understanding.

Psalm 120:1
"I took my troubles to the LORD; I cried out to Him, and He answered my prayer."

Amen

Day 284
October 11th

Stay Positive

Tonight, Lord we pray for the cowgirl who is working hard to stay positive. It doesn't mean she is without struggle. Instead, she chooses to find blessings in her burdens, to find joy in the struggle, and to seek truth in the turbulence. We pray You bring her peace and comfort if those efforts fall short. May she always know You are with her through it all.

Proverbs 31:25
"She is clothed with strength and dignity, and she laughs without fear of the future."

Amen

Day 285
October 12th

Step In

Tonight, Lord we pray for the cowgirl who needs You to step in. She needs You to take hold of a situation or person. Maybe it's a situation she's in the middle of or one that is out of her hands. If it's a person who needs Your hands of guidance, Lord, we pray You step in and knock on the door of their heart until they answer. She knows no situation is out of Your control, and so she knows it is safe with You. She prays for comfort in her own heart as she lays this burden at Your feet.

Psalm 32:8
"I will instruct you and teach you in the way you should go; I will counsel you with My loving eye on you."

Amen

Day 286
October 13th

Longing for the one

Lord, tonight we pray for our cowgirls seeking their cowboy partners. She spends her days working and building her future, praising You and giving You the glory for it all. The one thing that seems to be missing is someone else to share it with. She knows her worth and isn't going to settle for less. But sometimes the wait wears on her heart and the frogs she's met leave her discouraged. We pray she remembers that You are not only preparing her, but You are preparing the partner she needs. These things happen in Your timing not hers (or her mother's that keeps asking for grand-babies). May You grant her the patience to wait for the one You have prepared. And we pray she seeks to grow her relationship with You in her waiting.

Isaiah 30:18
"Yet the LORD longs to be gracious to you; therefore, He will rise up to show you compassion. For the LORD is a God of justice. Blessed are all who wait for Him!"

Amen

Day 287
October 14th

Tough Call

Lord, tonight we pray for the cowgirl making hard decisions. She may be making decisions for herself or her family. They may be decisions she wants to make or ones she's been avoiding. She sometimes struggles more with the outcome of hard decisions than actually making them- wondering if it was the right decision, or what others may think. We pray, Lord, You remind her of Your presence with her always. We pray she remembers no matter the decisions, You are in control, and she can always lean on You for comfort. May she seek Your guidance and direction for the right decisions, and may she find Your peace every step of the way.

Psalm 119:105
"Your word is a lamp to guide my feet and a light for my path."

Amen

Day 288
October 15th

Waves of Emotion

As we come to you tonight, Lord, we want to pray for the cowgirl struggling with a new or young horse. Oh, the rollercoaster of highs and lows can sure be humbling, Lord.
We know the plans You have for us, Lord, plans to prosper and not to harm, plans to give us hope and a future.

Jeremiah 29:11.
"We pray for You to guide our hands and minds to help mesh with our four-legged partner. May we praise You in the highs and seek You in the lows, and always be grateful for the opportunity."

Amen

Day 289
October 16th

Angels Among Us

Lord, tonight we pray for the cowgirls and their families who have passed on to You. We pray thanks for the wonderful blessings they were in our lives. We pray thanks over all the lives they touched and the families they raised. We also pray, Lord, for the cowgirls and family and friends left behind here on earth. We know our loved ones are welcomed by You, their pain is gone, and their bodies restored.
Knowing those things brings comfort to our hurting hearts. We pray for comfort and peace over any unanswered questions for we know Your plans are better, even if we don't understand. We pray thanks for the journey we shared with them and the memories we will always cherish. For we haven't truly lost someone when we know where they went.

John 16:22
"Now is your time of grief, but I will see you again and you will rejoice, and no one will take away your joy"

Amen

Day 290
October 17th

Searching for Your Village

Lord, tonight we pray for the cowgirl trying to find her place. It may be at a new job, a new barn, a new discipline, or a new town. Whatever the case, she just wants to find a place to belong. A place to feel like she fits. As cowgirls, Lord, we know we are born to stand out- to stand tall and brave in the face of adversity, to grow our confidence in who we are in You and through You. She knows this Lord and prays for You to remind her heart and to calm her mind when the doubts creep in. We also pray, Lord, she can find her groove and find her "people". The Christ-following cowgirl community is second to none, and we will lift each other up in prayer and helpful hands. We pray, Lord, You guide her steps and her heart to find her place in the newness and changes in her life. May she always know her place with You, Lord, and may she always find comfort in that.

2 Corinthians 13:14
"The grace of the Lord Jesus Christ and the love of God and the fellowship of the Holy Spirit be with you all."

Amen

Day 291
October 18th

Calloused Emotions

Lord, tonight we pray for the cowgirl who needs your peace and grace. She hasn't had it easy, Lord, and this life has probably hardened her heart a little. The race she runs is full of hurdles and she is tired. Tired of the disappointments, tired of lies and empty promises from people around her. We pray, Lord, for your grace to surround her when her frustrations get the better of her. We pray for peace, Lord, calm her soul and fill it with Your love. Remind her, Your promises never fail, and You will always show up when she needs You. May she find comfort in knowing You see the truth even through the lies of others.

Jeremiah 17:10
"I the LORD search the heart and test the mind, to give every man according to his ways, according to what their actions deserve."

Amen

Day 292
October 19th

Facing the inevitable

Lord, tonight we pray for the cowgirl facing a giant. It may physical, emotional, a troubled relationship, or just a giant situation. As David did Goliath, Lord, she knows it's a giant she must face, not only for herself, but for those around her. No matter the situation, Lord, we know she will need Your strength, guidance, and comfort. Regardless of the distance, the road won't be easy, so we pray she feels Your presence every step.

Psalm 18:2
"The LORD is my rock, my fortress, and my savior; my God is my rock, in whom I find protection. He is my shield, the power that saves me, and my place of safety."

Amen

Day 293
October 20th

Outside looking In

Lord, tonight we come to You to pray for the cowgirl feeling left out. We pray for the cowgirl who isn't sure where she fits in. Maybe it's at work where no one understands why she comes to work with hay in her hair. Maybe it's at school where she's been labeled the "weird horse girl". Maybe she feels like the newbie or novice at the barn or events. Whatever the case, Lord, we pray You bring her strength to persevere on the days that are tough. We pray You bring her peace in knowing the passion and talents she holds are gifts from You, handcrafted especially for her. We pray she finds her place and her people to feel welcomed. We pray, Lord, that when she has that, she takes notice when someone else feels left out. May she shine Your light and be the one to reach out.

1 Thessalonians 5:11
"Therefore encourage and comfort each other and build one another up"

Amen

Day 294
October 21st

An unexpected turn

Lord, tonight we pray for the cowgirl who feels like her plans have derailed, interrupted, or fallen flat. As a cowgirl, she is used to making plans and getting things done. There is too much on her plate not to make sure she has things lined out. But this also makes it hard when the visions and plans she had in her mind, don't match the reality she faces. We pray, Lord, that she takes time to remember all her plans that you have rerouted before. The missed turns that turned into opportunities and the heartache that turned into new blessings. Although she might not always understand the plans You have for her, Lord, she can always be sure they are better than her own plans. We pray she take pause to seek guidance for her steps. And we pray for comfort and grace for any growing pains along the way.

Proverbs 16:9
"A man's heart plans his course, but the LORD determines his steps."

Amen

Day 295
October 22nd

Undoubted Faith

Lord, tonight we pray for the cowgirl wishing she could have a glimpse into the future. Wishing she could know what is on the other side of this valley, she's stuck in or this mountain she's climbing. She doesn't doubt your plan. Lord, she just wishes she knew the next chapter. Somehow, she feels like that might make the hard steps a little easier. But she knows You called her to walk by faith and not sight. We pray you lift her head and fill her heart with strength. We pray she gain faith with each step as she moves forward on Your promises, Lord. Bring her comfort and grace on the days her feet get heavy. May she rejoice and give thanks as she sees Your plan unfold.

Ecclesiastes 3:11
"Yet God has made everything beautiful for its own time. He has planted eternity in the human heart, but even so, people cannot see the whole scope of God's work from beginning to end."

Amen

Day 296
October 23rd

His plan, not Yours

Lord, tonight we pray for the cowgirl who is in a season she doesn't understand. She takes steps in darkness on faith. These parts of her journey are the hardest to walk. She knows it is all a part of Your plan, Lord, so she prays for Your guidance. The obstacles she faces, the heartache and challenges coming her way, make her question lots of things. We pray, Lord, in those moments, she finds You close. Bring her comfort and peace in Your plan.

Proverbs 3: 5-6
"Trust in the LORD with all your heart and lean not on your own understanding; in all your ways acknowledge Him, and He will make your paths straight."

Amen

Day 297
October 24th

Expectations

Lord, tonight we pray for the cowgirl dealing with expectations. Whether it's her own expectations or someone else's, the trouble is they tend to argue with reality. Sometimes her own expectations can lead to disappointment. When that happens, Lord, we pray she seeks You for guidance. We pray she seeks You for peace and patience. May she seek Your truth and have clarity over the situation. If it's the expectations of others she battles, Lord, we pray for her to remember whose expectations really matter. We pray she remembers she is a daughter of the Lord, and that love is unconditional. In all things, we pray for Your hand of truth and clarity, Lord. Be with her and guide her steps.

Ephesians 3:20
"Now to him who is able to do far more abundantly than all that we ask or expect, according to the power at work within us."

Amen

Day 298
October 25th

Treading Water

Lord, tonight we pray for the cowgirl who needs Your hand- Your hand of guidance, Your hand of comfort, and Your hand of intervention. She feels a bit off course and isn't sure where to turn, so she's turning to you. The steps she's taken lately have been rocky; we pray You carry her to softer shores. Her days have been stress-filled not knowing which way to turn to get back on course. We pray Your comfort and direction cover her. And for the stubborn streak that runs through her, Lord, we pray You lay a firm hand of intervention over her misdirection. May she find it with an open heart and mind.

1 Peter 5:10
"After you have suffered, the God of all grace, who has called you to His eternal glory in Christ, will Himself restore you, secure you, strengthen you, and establish you."

Amen

Day 299
October 26th

Self Control

Lord, tonight we pray for the cowgirl who needs patience- More patience for Your plan, more patience for her family, more patience for her career, or more patience for Your timing. In a fast-paced world with a to-do list a mile long, sometimes it's hard to find patience. And a long day of obstacles tends to run it out faster. We pray, Lord, she seek You to find the peace that passes all understanding. The peace that brings her back to clarity in the chaos and allows her to find patience. We pray she remember nothing good comes when she loses her patience. May she find a deep breath and Your listening ear when she needs a moment to gather her thoughts. Surround her in Your mercy and grace!

Romans 12:12
"Rejoice in hope, be patient in tribulation, be constant in prayer"

Amen

Day 300
October 27th

Gratitude

Dear Lord, tonight we want to say thank you. Thanks, Lord, for sitting with us in the storm and quietly wrapping us in Your love and provision. Thanks Lord, for sending us Your love through friends, strangers, angels and through all the small things that mean the most. Thank you for constantly showing up in every way we need to You. Thanks Lord, for the complete and unyielding power of prayer. Thanks Lord, for the blessing that is committing all our fears to You, and knowing beyond a shadow of a doubt, that You have it all under control.

Psalms 91:11
"For He will command His angels concerning you to guard you in all your ways."

Amen

Day 301
October 28th

Unconditional Love

Dear Lord, tonight we pray for the cowgirl who is struggling with sin. Maybe it's her words or her thoughts, or maybe something more. Lord, help her to remember we've all sinned and fallen short. Bring wise counsel around her to speak truth over her life. The truth of who she is in Your eyes. Let her know that although she fails, she is never forgotten, and she is loved and forgiven. Let her see the truth in Your word and help her to believe her shortcomings and her sinful nature do not define her. Remind her she is the child of the One who leaves the 99, who welcomes her back to His love and mercy with open arms. And, if she would only decide to trust You, Lord, You will change her heart and help her grow closer to You in Your perfect love.

1 Corinthians 10:13
"No temptation has overtaken you except what is common to mankind. And God is faithful; he will not let you be tempted beyond what you can bear. But when you are tempted, he will also provide a way out so that you can endure it."

Amen

Day 302
October 29th

Blind Faith

Tonight Lord, we come to You to pray for the cowgirl who puts her faith over fear. The world says there are many things to fear, but she knows her faith lies in You. Still the evil in this world tries to push its way into her mind. When the world is too much, Lord, we pray she recites Your Word.

Psalm 118:6
"'The Lord is with me; I will not be afraid.' We pray as she speaks these words, she also feels You cover and shield her with your armor. Fill her spirit with Your strength and renew her faith."

Amen

Day 303
October 30th

Battling Solitude

Lord, tonight we pray for the cowgirl feeling alone. She may be surrounded by people, and yet she feels like no one quite understands how she feels. She greets those around her with a smile and kind words even if she feels broken inside. But when we look to Your Word Lord

Deuteronomy 31:8
"The LORD Himself goes before you; He will be with you. He will never leave you nor forsake you. Do not be afraid or discouraged."

We pray, Lord, that she reads this over and over until it sinks in and she feels it in her soul. May she feel Your blanket of peace cover her and surround her. We pray no matter the valley or darkness in which she walks, she feels Your presence and finds comfort.

Amen

Day 304
October 31st

Compassion

Lord, tonight we pray for the cowgirl who needs kindness. Sometimes the world we live in lacks in that department. She is silent about her daily struggles. But those struggles are a little bit tougher when others don't choose kindness. That combination makes it tough to choose kindness herself somedays. We pray, Lord, that she seek You and strive to love like You. We pray she remembers the grace You give her and that she chooses to extend that grace to others. We pray You fill her heart with Your unconditional love. May her heart overflow and spread to others.

Ephesians 4:32
"Be kind and tenderhearted to one another, forgiving each other just as in Christ God forgave you."

Amen

Day 305
November 1st

Self Criticism

Tonight, we pray for the cowgirl who needs to have a short memory. The ups and downs of life will come and go, but she will miss the ups if she gets stuck thinking about the downs. Opportunities are around every corner, but if she spends too much time replaying the should haves and the could haves, she won't see the can haves. We pray she finds strength in You to move forward after tough breaks. We pray You give her grace when things don't roll her way. We pray You bring her peace to know that You are always in control. At the end of the day, Lord, we pray that win or learn, she gives You all the glory and shines Your light in all she does.

Philippians 3:13,
"I have not achieved it, but I focus on this one thing: Forgetting the past and looking forward to what lies ahead."

Amen

Day 306
November 2nd

Born For This

Lord, tonight we pray for our cowgirls seeking their purpose. The one for which You have prepared her for as it says in

Ephesians 2:10,
"For we are God's handiwork, created in Christ Jesus to do good works, which God prepared in advance for us to do."

She may have found purpose in her role as a mother, rancher, wife, or in her career. But maybe she feels a calling that is bigger than her current situation. Maybe she feels a bit lost all together, and wonders what direction You have planned for her. Whatever the case, Lord, we pray she seeks You and looks inward. For the passion You have placed in her heart will lead her to a purpose You have for her. We pray she seeks You for strength as she takes these new steps. And we pray she shines a light toward You in all she does.

Amen

Day 307
November 3rd

Heavy Burdens

Lord, tonight we pray for the cowgirl carrying a heavy mental load. The kind that wears her out without taking a single step. The kind that keeps her up at night while her mind races. It may be something she's shared with others, or maybe something she's kept to herself. Whatever the situation, Lord, we pray for Your hand over her. We pray for Your peace to cover her like a blanket. We pray that as her mind runs, she puts You in the center of her thoughts. May she remember that with You at the center, she can give You control and find rest. We pray she gives You the burden to carry.

Mathew 11:28
"Then Jesus said, 'Come to me, all of you who are weary and carry heavy burdens, and I will give you rest.'"

Amen

Day 308
November 4th

Pressing On

Lord, tonight we pray for the cowgirl struggling to understand the season she is in. She knows this world is not without trials and that she can learn from each one, but she is struggling to see the lesson. She doesn't understand the message in the mess. She doesn't understand what You seek for her to learn. As she sinks to her knees when the burden gets too heavy, we pray You meet her there. We pray You give her comfort and peace to know You are with her. We pray she sees the ways she can shine Your light through her darkness. Guide her so she may draw strength through this trial and persevere. May she reach the other side with a greater understanding of Your love. We pray she find ways she can help others with the strength she has gained through her trials. In the meantime, Lord, we pray You shed Your grace and mercy over her and lift her to her feet one day at a time.

James 1: 3-4
"For you know that when your faith is tested, your endurance has a chance to grow. Let perseverance finish its work so that you may be mature and complete, not lacking anything."

Amen

Day 309
November 5th

Pushing Through

Lord, tonight we pray for the cowgirl with a hurt heart. Her faith is strong, but her smile is weak. The lows and disappointments have started to dig deeper. She tries to keep her focus on you through every bump in this rollercoaster, but sometimes she struggles to see past the darkness. We pray for Your grace, Lord, lift her up when her legs are weak. Fill her heart when it feels empty. May she remember that, even in the darkest valley, You are with her. Forgive her when the frustration gets the best of her. Remind her that Your plan is good even when she doesn't see it.

John 16:33
"I have told you all this so that you may have peace in Me. Here on earth, you will have many trials and sorrows. But take heart because I have overcome the world."

Amen

Day 310
November 6th

I am because you were

Lord, tonight we want to pray for the cowgirls who came before us, the ones who paved the way for the dreams we chase today. For the ones who were brave enough to push through to compete in an event or a level that had never been done. For the ones who didn't listen when their families told them being a cowgirl wasn't proper. And for the ones who've gone to You, Lord, leaving a legacy in their children's and grandchildren's hearts. We pray for guidance from You to carry on in their footsteps and be a light for You.

Proverbs 13:22
"A good person leaves an inheritance for their children's children"

Amen

Day 311
November 7th

Put on a Brave Front

Lord, tonight we pray for the cowgirl who is tired. She's tired of putting on a brave face, tired of smiling through the pain, and tired of being let down. She feels like she works hard to do right and be better, but some days she wonders if it matters. Lord. We pray You lift this cowgirl up from the lies that fill her ears. We pray You fill her heart with Your truth and love. We pray, Lord, she looks in the mirror and remembers she is a child of God and she is fearfully and wonderfully made. Breathe life into her confidence that she is never alone and You walk with her every step of the way.

Joshua 1:9.
"Be strong and courageous. Do not be afraid; do not be discouraged, for the Lord, Your God will be with you wherever you go."

May she rest in Your promise to always be with her.

Amen

Day 312
November 8th

Fear of the Unknown

Lord, tonight we pray for the cowgirl facing the unexpected. It may be an unexpected turn of events, or maybe something she planned wasn't what she expected. Sometimes this rollercoaster of life feels like it's more than she can handle. We pray, Lord, that in this situation she turn to You and let You guide her feet. May she seek You in her darkest hours and know You are always present. We pray You fill her soul with Your unconditional love. Remind her that nothing is unexpected in Your eyes, and You have laid out her steps before her. Give her grace and mercy along the way.

Deuteronomy 31:8
"The LORD himself goes before you and will be with you; He will never leave you nor forsake you. Do not be afraid; do not be discouraged."

Amen

Day 313
November 9th

Confidence

Tonight Lord, we pray for the cowgirl who is ready to move mountains. Her faith is strong, and her heart is focused on You. She has kept her eyes on You, Lord, and walked the path You have for her. She knows the goodness You have for her is greater than she can dream on her own. She longs to let her dreams soar and fly on Your wings, but she knows Your plans come in Your time, not hers. We pray, Lord, You continue to prepare her to bare much fruit. May she seek You in every step and keep her focus on You. Give her peace and guide her so that as Your plan unfolds in front of her, she will be ready to move those mountains.

Proverbs 16:3
"Commit your work to the LORD, and your plans will be established. The LORD has made everything for its purpose."

Amen

Day 314
November 10th

Pushing through Fear

Tonight, we pray for the cowgirl stepping out of her comfort zone. Maybe it's a new discipline, starting to haul her colt, or entering a big event. She's put in the hard work, and she knows she's prepared, but it's all a little different outside that comfort zone. We pray she trusts in the effort she has given, and You will guide her nervous steps. We pray, Lord, when she accomplishes those goals, she gives the glory to You.

Proverbs 21:31
"The horse is made ready for the day of battle, but victory rests with the Lord"

Amen

Day 315
November 11th

Freedom Defenders

Tonight, we pray for the cowgirls who are veterans or in the military. We pray for the cowgirl whose spouse, son, daughter, father, cousin, uncle, aunt or any other family member is a veteran or in the military. The scenario in the world right now is troublesome. We pray Your hand of protection for those in the middle of it. We seek Your peace for these cowgirls, and we pray for Your grace to cover them all. Lord, You know the questions and fear in their hearts. We pray You bring peace, answers, and protection.

2 Samuel 22:3-4
"My God, my rock, in whom I take refuge, my shield, and the horn of my salvation, my stronghold and my refuge, my savior; you save me from violence. I call upon the Lord, who is worthy to be praised, and I am saved from my enemies."

Amen

Day 316
November 12th

Waiting for the One

Lord, tonight we want to pray for the cowgirl waiting for her cowboy. She knows You have a man that can handle her strong will and meet her stubbornness with a grin. And she won't settle for a man she can out work. She may have kissed a few frogs, Lord, and she's a bit discouraged.

Proverbs 18:22
"He who finds a wife finds a good thing."

We remind her, Lord, that she is the prize and a treasure. A prize is meant to be won and a treasure meant to be found. We pray she keeps her focus on You, Lord, and builds her relationship with YOU. Because as You are preparing the cowboy to find her, Lord, You are preparing her to be found. ♥

Amen

Day 317
November 13th

Give it to God

Lord, tonight we pray for the cowgirl who needs to lay it at Your feet. She's holding on tight- fighting, working, stressing over something that isn't meant for her to hold. She needs to let go and let God. She needs to turn over the weight she keeps trying to carry. She needs to stop trying to fit a square peg into a round hole. What is meant to come her way will come, if You will it, Lord. We pray she finds peace in knowing she doesn't have to have all the answers and she doesn't have to fight all the fights. Remind her that the real battle is already won. Give her grace and mercy and let her find peace in Your promises.

Psalm 55:22
"Cast your cares on the LORD and He will sustain you; He will never let the righteous be shaken."

Amen

Day 318
November 14th

In a Bind

Lord, tonight we pray for the cowgirl who finds herself in a mess. The kind that takes Your hand to sort out. We pray You lay Your hand of comfort, grace, and healing over any mess she has. When life gets messy, it's easy to throw our hands up and feel lost, but we know if we turn to You, You will always be there.

Ephesians 6: 10-11
"Be strong in the Lord, and in the power of His might. Put on the whole armor of God."

So we pray, Lord, that she puts on Your armor so she may face all that comes her way as she works through what lays ahead.

Amen

Day 319
November 15th

New Chapter

Lord, tonight we pray for the cowgirl in transition. Just as the leaves start to fall and the daylight shortens, she is in a season of change. She may be growing up and seeing changes in her own self. She may have outgrown the small bubble she felt comfortable in. She may simply be transitioning herself and her family for the things that cooler weather brings. Whatever the case, Lord, we pray she remembers to find Joy in the journey. We pray she remembers to take pause and see the beauty in the moments that will never come again. We pray You give her grace and comfort if this transition comes with difficulty. We pray You be her guide when her footsteps feel lost. And just as all seasons pass, we remind her so will this one. Give her grace, bring her peace, and be her guide.

Daniel 2:21
"He changes times and seasons; He removes kings and sets up kings; He gives wisdom to the wise and knowledge to those who have understanding; He reveals deep and hidden things; He knows what is in the darkness, and the light dwells with Him."

Amen

Day 320
November 16th

Burnt out

Lord, tonight we pray for the cowgirl needing a recharge. Her busy life drained her and time to rest doesn't seem too near in the future. Between work, livestock, and family, someone or something always needs her time or energy. She is thankful for these things, and she counts them as blessings, not burdens. But her energy doesn't seem to match the demand. We pray, Lord, for her to "plug" in to You and recharge her passion and her purpose. Fill her tank and restore her drive. And most importantly, Lord, as she lays her head down tonight, we pray You release her worries and her stressors so she may find rest in You.

Mathew 11:28
"Come to Me, all you who are weary and burdened, and I will give you rest."

Amen

Day 321
November 17th

Family Conflict

Tonight Lord, we pray for the cowgirl who needs prayers for family. It may be a new feud or a fire that's burned for a while, but it hurts just the same. She longs for the opportunity to put the situation behind them and move forward. But one thing or another keeps coming around to bring back the hurt feelings. Tonight, we pray for each side to see forgiveness in their hearts. May we forgive as You forgive, and may we love the way You love us. If she is at fault, Lord, we pray she asks for forgiveness, and if she has been wronged, we pray she forgives even without request. We know this is the first step in healing, and that is what we seek Lord.

Matthew 6:14
"Forgive other people when they sin against you, your heavenly Father will also forgive you."

Amen

Day 322
November 18th

Beating yourself up

Lord, tonight we pray for the cowgirl who needs to cut herself some slack and not be so hard on herself. She can be her own worst critic no matter the situation and she has a hard time forgiving herself. Sometimes, she finds it easier to forgive others than herself. That wears on her heart. Eventually, too many harsh words spoken internally will make their way to her heart and mind. We pray, Lord, You remind her Your forgiveness is all she needs to ask for and Your love is unconditional. We pray no matter what it is she is criticizing herself for, You trust and believe in her. May she seek You for guidance and comfort. We pray You speak truth into her heart and comfort her mind. Remind her and cover her in Your unconditional love.

Romans 5:5
"This hope will not lead to disappointment. For we know how dearly God loves us, because He has given us the Holy Spirit to fill our hearts with His love."

Amen

Day 323
November 19th

Appreciate the journey

Lord, tonight we pray for the cowgirl who is living her dream. She's thankful for every ounce of blood sweat and tears that brought her to where she is today. She's thankful for every step taken of this journey. Whether she is in the highlight reel of her dream or still battling in the trenches, she knows every opportunity is one to be thankful for. And every opportunity comes with a responsibility. A responsibility to shine a light for You, to walk in Your grace, and show Your goodness. We pray, Lord, that she continues to seek You, and You continue to guide her toward her dreams to fulfill the passion You placed in her heart.

Colossians 3:23
"Whatever you do, work at it with all your heart, as working for the Lord."

Amen

Day 324
November 20th

People Pleasing

Tonight, we pray for the cowgirl with too much on her plate, Lord. She has trouble saying no when others ask for help. She has plenty of her own projects and problems, but she hates the thought of letting someone down by not lending a hand. She spreads herself too thin and ultimately something breaks. It may be her patience or her promises, but in the end, it's her heart. Lord, we ask You to surround her servant's heart with comfort and help her build healthy boundaries. Guide her to find a balance and a good plan, and instead of "no" perhaps she can say, "maybe tomorrow". Tonight, Lord, take her heavy load and give her peace to know she can turn it over to You.

2 Corinthians 1:3-4
"Blessed be the God and Father of our Lord Jesus Christ, the Father of mercies and God of all comfort, who comforts us in all our affliction, so that we may be able to comfort those who are in any affliction, with the comfort with which we ourselves are comforted by God."

Amen

Day 325
November 21st

Delayed Gratification

Tonight Lord, we pray for the cowgirls trying to work hard for the next generation. It may be her own kiddos or the neighbor's kids that ride their bike to help around the farm. She strives to lead by example, to show how hard work pays off, how big goals sometimes take time and patience. She sees this crazy world turn on itself more each day and she worries what will be left after she's gone. She prays and works each day to keep a way of life alive.
A way of hard honest work, a way of prayer and praise through every triumph and trial. Be with her as she sets an example and prays to be a light toward You.

Proverbs 22:6
"Train up a child in the way he should go; even when he is old, he will not depart from it."

Amen

Day 326
November 22nd

Tough Decisions

Lord, we come to You tonight for the cowgirl whose heart is torn. She splits her time, her energy, or her goals. She works so hard to make it all work in unison, but at the end of the day, something has to give. She's forced to pick between the things she needs or wants to do and everything in between. The new baby is such a blessing, but her colts sit idle. She's finally landed that new job, but she's thinking of selling her good horse because she doesn't have the time to compete anymore. The choices of a cowgirl aren't always fun, Lord, but we pray she turns to You for Your guidance. We know You have the perfect plan. You have a way of working things out. Guide her heart in the direction of peace, Lord.

2 Corinthians 4:8-9
"We are pressed on every side by troubles, but we are not crushed. We are perplexed, but not driven to despair. We are hunted down, but never abandoned by God. We get knocked down, but we are not destroyed.

Amen

Day 327
November 23rd

Clean Slate

Tonight Lord, we pray for the cowgirl who is starting over. It may be a job, a relationship, a new horse, or a new place to call home. She may have taken a leap of faith to get here, or she may have been pushed until she jumped. Whatever the case, Lord, her heart fills with anticipation, worry, excitement, and/or fear. A change like this comes with a lot of emotions that can be hard to navigate. Lord, we pray You be her guide, and we pray You be her sounding board to turn over her worries. Give her strength when she feels unsure about the next step. Remind her the journey ahead isn't alone, and You will be with her each step.

Proverbs 3:5-6
"Trust in the Lord with all your heart and do not lean on your own understanding. In all your ways, acknowledge Him, and He will make your paths straight."

Amen

Day 328
November 24th

Overwhelming Tasks

Lord, tonight we pray for the cowgirl trying to catch up. Life gets busier by the day, and it doesn't seem to be slowing down. It may be house and barn work, bills, kids, or relationships. Somedays she's trying to catch up to those around her; other days, she's just hoping to catch a break. When she catches up on one thing, another falls behind. We pray, Lord, You give her grace and know that You see all her effort. Restore her faith in herself and cover her in Your peace. May she remember You are in control and that You walk with her each step of the way.

Joshua 1:9
"Be strong and courageous. Do not be frightened, and do not be dismayed, for the Lord your God is with you wherever you go."

Amen

Day 329
November 25th

Grateful for Guidance

Lord, tonight we pray for the cowgirl who is just thankful for the opportunity. Whether she is winning or learning, been living the dream for years or just getting started. Her dreams are big and the passion behind them is bigger. She prays for Your guidance and direction because she knows the passion in her heart came from You. She knows Your plans for her exceed any she has for herself. She is thankful for every door You open and every opportunity You provide. May she walk through and seize each one with the faith in her heart that can move mountains.

Psalm 32:8
"I will instruct you and teach you in the way you should go; I will counsel you with My eye upon you."

Amen

Day 330
November 26th

Refiner's Fire

Lord, tonight we come to you for the cowgirl who feels like she's under fire. Not the trial by fire kind, but the refiner's fire.

Zechariah 13:9
"I will bring that group through the fire and make them pure. I will refine them like silver and purify them like gold. They will call on My name, and I will answer them. I will say, 'These are My people,' and they will say, 'The LORD is our God.'"

Though uncomfortable, it's the kind of fire she knows is making her better. It may be with relationships, her job, her livestock, or her parenting. No matter the situation, Lord, we pray she remembers You are in control and working all things for her good. Just as a refiner works to turn out the beauty we see in silver and gold, You, Lord, are working her for better things ahead, so she may be strong and shine bright as a symbol of Your love and direction. We pray she finds comfort in knowing the beauty You see in her Lord.

Amen

Day 331
November 27th

Inadequate

Tonight, Lord we come to you to pray for the cowgirl who doesn't feel like she is enough. Whether it's in her work, a relationship, or the arena, she feels like she comes up short. Short of her own expectations or what others may expect of her. The truth is, Lord, most of the time she hasn't really come up short at all. We pray, Lord, you give her Grace when she feels like she has fallen short. We pray You bring her peace and comfort when she feels she isn't enough. And we pray You bring her strength and remind her that with You and through You all things are possible. Your strength is made perfect in weakness and so we pray that she relinquishes the control she thinks she has, to give You power over her life. May she look in the mirror and see herself as You see her. Perfectly and wonderfully made in Your image. A child of the most high King. May she see her reflection and know in Your eyes she is always enough, and nothing will change that.

Hebrews 10:35
"So do not throw away this confident trust in the Lord. Remember the great reward it brings you!"

Amen

Day 332
November 28th

Unconditional Love

Tonight Lord, we pray for the cowgirl who sings Your praise. She gives You praise even when her heart doesn't understand. She gives You praise when the world tells her she worked hard to earn it. And she gives You praise in all the little victories along the way. The hills and valleys in her journey don't always follow her plan and she doesn't always understand all the why's. But what she does understand is Your love is never-ending and Your truth never fails. Those things, she has learned, are praise-worthy, even on her hardest days. She knows even on her best days, nothing she does would be possible without Your saving grace. So, pray for her peace and comfort on those tough days. We pray for guidance to be a light for You in all she does.

John 16:33
"I have told you these things, so that in Me you may have peace. In this world you will have trouble. But take heart because I have overcome the world."

Amen

Day 333
November 29th

Maternal Obligations

Lord, tonight we pray for our cowgirl mommas. She's trying to find balance, direction, and grace. She may work a 9-5 and care for everything else in between or she may keep the whole ship running around the clock. She's lost count of the irons in the fire and just prays nothing goes up in flames. She prays for guidance to find the balance between all the hats she wears. Cover her in grace and mercy on the days she feels like she's fallen short. Remind her she is not alone in any of her struggles.

Psalm 46:5
"God is within her, she will not fall".

Amen

Day 334
November 30th

Holiday Apprehension

Lord, tonight we pray for the cowgirl who struggles during the holidays. Maybe it's the stress that comes with the busyness of the season or tight finances causing a strain. Maybe she's feeling the loss of someone now missing at family gatherings. Whatever the case, Lord, we pray that she step back and find joy in the real reason for Christmas. May she find peace in the promise of the Savior. We pray she finds strength and remember the battle has already been won. Although the stresses and loss will still find a heavy place in her heart, we pray You cover her in a blanket of Your unconditional love.

Colossians 3:15
"And let the peace of Christ rule in your hearts, to which also you were called in one body. And be thankful."

Amen

Day 335
December 1st

Closure

Lord, tonight we for the cowgirl preparing to say goodbye. It may be goodbye to a job, goodbye to her hometown, goodbye to a friend moving, or the final goodbye to a loved one. As a rule, goodbyes don't generally come easy, but this one seems particularly hard. She will cherish the memories made and hold them close. We pray, Lord, You comfort her and guide her as she navigates this part of her journey. We pray You bring her strength and grace to help dry her eyes when the tears come. Bring her peace to know she can lay this hurt at Your feet You will carry it for her and never leave her.

John 16:22
"Now is your time of grief, but I will see you again and you will rejoice, and no one will take away your joy."

Amen

Day 336
December 2nd

Losing Sight

Tonight Lord, we pray for the cowgirl who needs some direction. She has lots of plans, ideas and goals, but she's missing the pieces that fit them together. They don't quite add up to this journey she's on and she feels more like she's wandering. Maybe she needs to sit down and reevaluate some things, or maybe she just needs to be more focused. But tonight, Lord, we pray she takes a step back to make sure her all these ideas and plans line up with a relationship with You. Because sometimes, we feel most lost on our journey when we have strayed from our walk with You, Lord. But when that relationship is strengthened, the path narrows, and the fog clears to reveal the road ahead. So tonight, we pray as she comes to You, You take her by the hand to see her through the steps ahead.

Proverbs 3:5-6
"Trust in the Lord with all thine heart; and lean not unto thine own understanding. In all thy ways acknowledge Him, and He shall direct thy paths".

Amen

Day 337
December 3rd

Self Preservation

Tonight Lord, we pray for the cowgirl who needs to be washed clean. Washed clean of her worries, her fears, and her anxieties. Washed clean of her past, her hurt, and her mistakes. We pray You wash away all of the lies, heartache, and doubts that have held her captive. We pray You restore her, body, mind and soul. We pray You bring her peace in knowing You already paid the ultimate price and through You, she has salvation. May that peace wash over her and restore her faith.

Isaiah 12:2
"Behold, God is my salvation, I will trust and not be afraid; For the LORD GOD is my strength and song, And He has become my salvation."

Amen

Day 338
December 4th

Spread Thin

Lord, tonight we pray for the cowgirl needing your Grace. Her days are so full and the to-do list never ends. She finds herself not taking time for You and Your Word, Lord. Many days, she feels unworthy as she falls short. Her patience runs thin and her temper short. Each and every day she needs Your grace. On these days, Lord, we pray You cover her in it. We pray You meet her right where she is, Lord, fixing fence, feeding babies, filing papers, or feeding livestock. May she feel Your unconditional love surround her and reassure her.

Hebrews 4:16
"Let us then approach God's throne of grace with confidence, so that we may receive mercy and find grace to help us in our time of need."

Amen

Day 339
December 5th

Discouraged

Tonight Lord, we pray for the cowgirl who needs to see You. She needs to see You in whatever situation she's in. She needs to see You give clarity to her chaos. She needs to see You heal the hurt. She needs to see You give peace in the pain. She knows Your plans are better, Lord, but right now she doesn't see it. She may not have the words right now, Lord, so we pray You hear her heart. We pray for You to show up and show her Your grace. We pray big prayers tonight, Lord, for peace, healing, and grace. May she see You in Your word.

Psalm 34:18
"The LORD is close to the brokenhearted; He rescues those whose spirits are crushed."

Amen

Day 340
December 6th

Seeking Solidity

Lord, tonight we pray for our cowgirls who are worn out. Whether it's sleepless nights with babies, hours with vets for sick animals, or bills that outrun the income. She is worn thin. Her patience, her ambition, and her peace are all running on empty. We pray, Lord, You lift her up and bring her Your strength to persevere. We pray You bring her peace to know You are in control and she is not in this alone. Lord, we pray You give her grace when she falls short. May she seek You for guidance to weather this storm. This too shall pass, easier days are ahead, and we pray You comfort her in this struggle.

Psalm 91:4
"He will cover you with His feathers. He will shelter you with His wings. His faithful promises are your armor and protection."

Amen

Day 341
December 7th

Mending Relationships

Tonight Lord, we pray for the cowgirl working through a strained relationship. It may be family or friends; it may be a boss or coworker. Relationships, no matter the depth or circumstance, aren't always easy. When they hit a snag, it can be even more difficult to find the right patch. There are always two sides to everything. And those two sides come with separate emotions and perspectives. We pray, Lord, whatever the scenario, You give them grace and You remind them of the power of forgiveness. We pray for open minds and open hearts to find forgiveness and resolution, Lord.

Ephesians 4:32
"Be kind to one another, tenderhearted, forgiving one another, as God in Christ forgave you."

Amen

Day 342
December 8th

Seeking Stability

Lord, tonight we pray for the cowgirl who needs to turn it over to You. She has so many irons in the fire and plates she's juggling, she struggles to keep up. Others look at her and wonder how she keeps it all together. The truth is, on the inside she feels like she's falling apart. She feels like she's one stumbling step from falling; one wrong turn from turning around. We pray, Lord, she lay it at Your feet. We pray You lift the burden from her weary shoulders, bring peace to her busy mind. Remind her, You will take the reins and comfort her she need only to hand them over.

Psalm 55:22
"Cast your burden upon the LORD and He will sustain you; He will never let the righteous be shaken."

May she read those words and embrace them with Your authority to empower her to let go. May she feel the burdens lift as she releases each one to You.

Amen

Day 343
December 9th

Seeking Grace

Tonight Lord, we pray for the cowgirl who needs patience. It may be the stress of the holidays. Maybe she's reflecting on a year of goals left unchecked. This time of year can be hard, Lord. This season is full of busyness and all the hustle and bustle can add stress to the days. We pray instead, she seeks joy and the real reason for the season. For the cowgirls reflecting on the year, we pray she remembers that the new year will bring new opportunity. We pray she seeks strength for patience to trust in Your plan.

Romans 12:12
"Rejoice in hope, be patient in trials, be constant in prayer."

Amen

Day 344
December 10th

Developmental Potential

Lord, tonight we pray for the cowgirls starting something new. It may be a new horse, discipline, job, or relationship. Each brings so much joy for all the things You have in store for her and this new journey. However, new things also mean change and change can be uncomfortable, Lord. We pray she sees these changes as opportunities to grow, opportunities to progress in this new journey.

Isaiah 43:19
"See, I am doing a new thing! Now it springs up; do you not perceive it? I am making a way in the wilderness and streams in the wasteland."

Lord, we pray she remembers You are in control and she can rest all her worries on You and take on this new journey!

Amen

Day 345
December 11th

Restore Life

Lord, tonight we come to You to pray for the cowgirl who needs to get through one more day. She feels like she's at the end of her rope and doesn't know where to turn. She needs to ease her pain; she needs to feel the weight lift; she needs to rest her mind. We pray, Lord, You lift her soul, revive her spirit and help her push through one more day, one day at a time. One step in front of the other toward healing and happiness. We pray, Lord, she realizes she doesn't have to have it all figured out today. We pray she understands she doesn't have to know it all right now, because You already do! We pray she remembers that You hold all her tomorrows and You are working on them for her good. We pray she releases her worries to You and lets You carry her through one day at a time. May she rely on You to bring her through the valley and may she rejoice with You on the other side.

Jeremiah 29:11
"'For I know the plans I have for you,' declares the Lord, 'plans to prosper you and not to harm you, plans to give you a hope and a future.'"

Amen

Day 346
December 12th

Weary Soul

Lord, tonight we pray for the cowgirl who is running on empty. Emotionally, physically, and every emotion in between. Whether it's the animals, work, or her family, someone always needs something. Somedays she doesn't even remember what her own plans were because something else pushed them out of her priorities. We pray, Lord, she takes a pause. A pause to remind herself of all the blessings surrounding her. We pray she takes that moment to stop and breathe. We pray she soaks up Your love and You fill her cup. May she take the time to remember that she is not alone and that You are always with her.

Psalm 46:5
"God is within her; she will not be moved. God will help her when morning dawns."

Amen

Day 347
December 13th

Prioritizing

Lord, tonight we pray for the cowgirl who needs to finish what she started. Maybe it's a new project, maybe it's a goal she has been working toward, or maybe it's a colt sitting on the back-burner. Sometimes she gets a wild hair and starts a lot of projects only to find them half-finished down the road. Tonight, we pray she focuses on her commitments big or small. We pray You guide her thoughts and steps toward bigger things. We pray, as she finishes each task, that she gives You the glory for the strength and perseverance.

Psalm 37:5
"Commit everything You do to the LORD. Trust Him, and He will help you."

Amen

Day 348
December 14th

Placing it in His Hands

Lord, tonight we pray for the cowgirl laying her heart in Your plans. Her dreams, her goals, all the work she has put in is nothing without Your hand. She prays that You guide her, protect her, and give her grace. She puts her faith in You and knows Your plans are always greater no matter the outcome. We pray for clarity and direction. May she seek You and give You all the glory win or learn. We pray she find joy in the journey every step of the way.

Psalm 33:11
"But the plans of the LORD stand firm forever, the purposes of His heart through all generations."

Jeremiah 29:11
"For I know the plans I have for you," declares the LORD, "plans to prosper you and not to harm you, plans to give you hope and a future."

Amen

Day 349
December 15th

Overcoming Adversity

Lord, tonight we pray for the cowgirl who is overcoming struggles. She stands on the other side thankful for the opportunities in front of her, and thankful for the trials behind her. She has worked to find joy in the journey and even on her hardest days she still finds peace in You. She knows the road ahead won't always be easy, but we pray she's learned lessons through the dark days behind her. We pray healing as she continues to overcome the wounds of her past. We pray guidance, as we know the journey ahead isn't without speed bumps. For the cowgirl still in the valley, we pray she feel Your comfort guide her through to the other side. As Your light and love fill her heart, Lord, we pray she use it to shine and show others the way to You.

James 1:12
"Blessed is the one who perseveres under trial because, having stood the test, they will receive the crown of life that the Lord has promised to those who love Him."

Amen

Day 350
December 16th

Heavy Burden

Lord, tonight we pray for the cowgirl who has more projects than she has time. So much to do, so little time as the saying goes. Somedays, she gets overwhelmed at even the thought of where to start. Other days, she has a perfect plan to accomplish so much, and the plan goes off the rails. She's left with her head in her hands, and nothing checked off the list. These days, she's left feeling discouraged and more overwhelmed than when she started. Lord, we pray for peace. Peace to know You are in control, peace to know that it all will work out in Your timing. We pray for clarity; let her see through the fog of her overwhelming thoughts. We pray she remembers no amount of worry or stress will lessen the list in front of her. May she take her new-found peace and clarity and find a path for progress one step at a time.

Matthew 6:34
"Therefore do not worry about tomorrow, for tomorrow will worry about itself."

Amen

Day 351
December 17th

The Weight of the World

Lord, tonight we pray for the cowgirl trying to be all the things. She wears many hats, has full plates, and still has irons in the fire. She feels like she is a "jack of all trades, master of none". There simply isn't enough of her to go around, Lord. The moment she puts her focus and energy into one thing another needs attention. To fully accomplish one thing, she must still balance all the others. Lord, we come to You for Your grace and mercy. We pray You wrap her in them, Lord. We pray You remind her You created all she is meant to be, and You do not make mistakes. Remind her when she feels like she is in a fight, that the battle has already been won. We pray You show her rest and bring her peace as she follows Your plan. Reassure her in the valleys, Lord, You walk with her and she is never alone. We pray, Lord, that even on her busiest days, she come to You and find rest.

Mathew 11:28
"Then Jesus said, "Come to me, all of you who are weary and carry heavy burdens, and I will give you rest."

Amen

Day 352
December 18th

Longing for Peace

Lord, tonight we pray for our cowgirls who need peace. This world has given her a rough go lately and she feels a little rattled. She clings to Your Word, and she knows Your promise to never leave her. Still, she finds her mind racing for answers when there are none to be found. She seeks Your peace Lord, the calm that washes over a soul that only You can provide, Lord. Tonight Lord, as she closes her eyes and comes to You, we pray You hold her close and reassure her pacing mind. We pray she feel Your presence and it brings her the relief she seeks. We pray she remembers You are in control of all the circumstances that surround her and when she reads these words, they echo in her soul.

Deuteronomy 31:8
"The Lord himself goes before you and will be with you; He will never leave you nor forsake you. Do not be afraid; do not be discouraged."

Amen

Day 353
December 19th

Feeling Drained

Lord, tonight we pray for the cowgirl who is tired. It may be physically, mentally, or emotionally and some days feel like all of them wrapped into one. The thing about cowgirls, though, is they tend not to come with an off switch. When there is work to do, you can bet she is all-in until the job's done. Whether it's fixing fence in the rain, doctoring animals in the freezing cold, or organizing bills and paperwork that keep the whole operation afloat. And it doesn't end when she hits the bed, Lord. Her mind continues to cross the t's and dot the i's of the day. We pray, Lord, You give her peace to know You see her and all the work she puts in each day. Meet her right where she is Lord and cover her in Your grace when the weight of the days get heavy. Give her the comfort and remind her she can lay it all at Your feet and rest her weary mind.

Exodus 33:14
"My Presence will go with you, and I will give you rest."

Amen

Day 354
December 20th

Needing Certainty

Lord, tonight we pray for the cowgirl seeking truth. In a world where it feels like you can't trust much of what you hear or read, she just needs truth. She needs something to believe in, something she can trust. She may be struggling with current events, a relationship, or something else that has caused her to lose faith in finding the truth. We pray, Lord, You remind her she can always seek You and Your Word to find the truth she needs. May she return to Your Word to find forgiveness to resolve conflict and mistrust.

John 8:32
"Then you will know the truth, and the truth will set you free."

Amen

Day 355
December 21st

Strength to Let Go

Tonight Lord, we pray for the cowgirl needing help to let go. It may mean to let go of a relationship that's not in her best interest. It may be to let go of her idea of how her life should go. Maybe she needs to let go of the apology she never got. Maybe she just needs to let go of the control she thinks she needs to keep. Lord, we pray she sees the purpose of letting go of things that hold her back. Things that keep her from a full and fulfilling future. These things take space in her heart and mind. We pray she finds the strength to see the reward in releasing them to You. With a mind and heart clear of these things, she can focus on you, Lord. We pray she gives herself that chance tonight and turns over to You, Lord. Let go and Let God.

Ecclesiastes 3:6
"A time to seek, and a time to lose; a time to keep, and a time to cast away."

Amen

Day 356
December 22nd

Covered in His Love

Lord, tonight we pray for the cowgirl who needs your love, Your unconditional never- ending love. She spends her days working hard for her family and her livelihood. She juggles all the plates and holds the pieces together. Sometimes she just needs reminding that Your love doesn't come with a to-do list for the day. She need only hold You close in her heart, close her eyes take pause and listen for Your guidance. In her stillness, Lord, we pray she feels Your love cover her like a blanket. With no questions asked, may the peace that passes all understanding fall over her like a blanket.

Isaiah 54:10
"Though the mountains move, and the hills shake, My love will not be removed from you and My covenant of peace will not be shaken," says your compassionate LORD."

Amen

Day 357
December 23rd

Settle for a Slowdown

Lord, tonight we pray for the cowgirl wishing she could hit fast forward. She wishes she could see the future ahead. She feels stuck in a moment she knows won't last forever, but she finds herself wishing it away. She knows she needs to push through, and she prays for Your guidance. Lord, only You may know what troubles her heart and makes her long to push past. We pray You bring her the peace that only You can provide. We pray even though she wants to hit fast forward, she hits pause if only to look to You and pray for comfort. May she take that moment to take a breath and feel Your peace and try to find joy in the journey of it all. We pray You guide her heart and her thoughts to the other side.

2 Peter 3:9
"The Lord is not slow in keeping His promise as some understand slowness, but is patient with you, not wanting anyone to perish but everyone to come to repentance."

Amen

Day 358
December 24th

The night before

Lord, tonight we come to you to pray thanks for you. On this Christmas Eve, we pray the cowgirl takes pause to soak in the beautiful gift that was the birth of Jesus Christ. We pray thanks for the gift of a Savior. We pray she is reminded of all the moments throughout the year you have provided comfort, grace, and peace. And for the Cowgirl who is struggling through this holiday season, we pray You bring her that same comfort, peace and grace. As we are reminded of your great gift, Lord, we pray to find ways to shine a light for You, Lord. May we be the body of Christ and give to and serve those around us to be Your light.

Luke 2:10-11
"And the angel said unto them, Fear not: for, behold, I bring you good tidings of great joy, which shall be to all people. For unto you is born this day in the city of David a Savior, which is Christ the Lord."

Amen

Day 359
December 25th

The Birth of Our Savior

Lord, tonight we pray for the cowgirl wrapping up this Christmas day. A busy day filled with presents and people. Chores and cooking, kids and chaos has her cup overflowing. With all the busyness and blessings, Lord, we pray she take a moment to look to You and pray thanks over all the things filling her day. For the cowgirl that has had a tough holiday, we pray You bring her comfort and peace. For her, it may have been a holiday of loneliness and loss. We pray You fill her heart with Your unconditional love. On this holy and precious day, we also pray thanks for the gift of a Savior.

Luke 19:10
"For the Son of Man came to seek and to save the lost."

Amen

Merry Christmas!

Day 360
December 26th

He Knows Your Heart

Lord, tonight we pray for the cowgirl's unanswered prayers and the answers to prayers never spoken. We pray thanks for all the times You provided what she needed instead of what she wanted. We pray thanks for all the times You prepared her for her true blessing in Your timing instead of what she asked for in the moment. We pray thanks over the protection You provide when we didn't know we needed it. We pray thanks over the times You guided our steps to a path greater than we knew possible. We pray thanks for a God that knows our past, present, and future and provides in each step of our journey. We pray thanks for the days that could have gone so wrong but didn't. Yet when we take a step back, we see Your guiding hand at every turn. Lord, we take for granted a lot of Your blessings, because we are too busy and preoccupied to see them. We pray, at the end of the day, we pause to look closer and see Your presence in all our steps. May we give thanks for all the grace and mercy You provide each and every day.

Proverbs 19:21
"Many plans are in a man's heart, but the purpose of the LORD will prevail."

Amen

Day 361
December 27th

Closing of a Chapter

Lord, tonight we pray for the cowgirl, full of emotions, headed into the last week of the year. Part of her can't help but think of the goals and the boxes left unchecked. Part of her is ready for a clean slate that the new year brings. We pray, Lord, that she takes this last week to make amends with what she can't take into the new year. We pray she finds joy in the journey of the past year. May she find strength in the things she's learned and prepare herself for the journey ahead. We pray Lord that she seek You for guidance and direction. We pray You bring her peace as she prepares to close one chapter and begin another. May she seek to grow closer to You and shine Your light brighter in the new year.

Psalm 65:11
"You crown the year with Your bounty, and Your paths overflow with plenty."

Amen

Day 362
December 28th

Overpowered

Lord, tonight we pray for the cowgirl feeling stuck. She may feel stuck in a job, a relationship, or a situation that feels out of her control. She wants to break free; she wants change, and she wants to feel like she has a choice. She feels broken, beaten and tired. She feels overwhelmed and backed in a corner. We pray for strength; we pray for clarity; we pray for direction. Lord, Your Word says

Hebrew 12: 1-2
"Therefore, since we are surrounded by so great a cloud of witnesses, let us also lay aside every weight, and sin which clings so closely, and let us run with endurance the race that is set before us, looking to Jesus, the founder and perfecter of our faith, who for the joy that was set before Him endured the cross, despising the shame, and is seated at the right hand of the throne of God."

We pray, Lord, You silence the lies she has led herself to believe; we pray You tear away the chains she feels upon herself, and we pray You breathe the life of truth back into her soul. Lord bring her the wisdom to seek truth, guidance, and the path you have for her.

Amen

Day 363
December 29th

Fuel your passion

Lord, tonight we pray thanks for the passion You placed in the cowgirl's heart. The passion to live a dream that requires blood, sweat, tears, long nights, and lonely miles. No matter the work that comes with it, she is grateful for every opportunity along the way. We pray thanks for the doors You have opened, the friends she's made, and Your guidance on every step of the journey. We pray, Lord, she continues to seek You through the passion You placed in her heart. And pray for Your grace and guidance when she walks astray. May she use her passion, gifts, and talents to shine a light for Your glory Lord.

Ephesians 2:10
"For we are God's workmanship, created in Christ Jesus to do good works, which God prepared in advance as our way of life."

Amen

Day 364
December 30th

Your own journey

Lord, tonight we pray for the cowgirl seeking guidance. She feels a bit lost, a bit confused, and a little overwhelmed. She sees big things working out for others and wonders where she went wrong. We pray she remembers everyone's journey is different and Your plan for her is as unique as the gifts you've given her to accomplish it. We pray she close her eyes and be still to allow You the control over her life and to guide her.

Psalm 46:10
"Be still, and know that I am God."

We pray she would feel your peace and grace fall over her and make way in her life.

Amen

Day 365
December 31st

New Goals Ahead

Lord, tonight we pray for the cowgirl ready for a new year. She is ready for a fresh start, new opportunities, new goals, and a clean slate. She prays her past mistakes and troubles stay behind her and for the chance to make things better. We pray for Your forgiveness and unconditional love to cover her as she steps into this new year. We pray You renew her faith and strength as she seeks to take on a fresh start. We pray Your guidance and direction over her.

Isaiah 43:18-19
"Do not call to mind the former things, or consider things of the past. For I am about to do something new. See, I have already begun! Do you not see it? I will make a pathway through the wilderness. I will create rivers in the dry wasteland."

Amen

Subject Index

Please enjoy this special index to find specific prayers relating to topics on your heart.

Feeling Stuck	Discouraged	Rough Road
Day 19	Day 77	Day 67
Day 109	Day 94	Day 115
Day 250	Day 158	Day 218
Day 362	Day 237	Day 312
Joy In the Journey	**Horse**	**Gods Plan**
Day 1	Day 3	Day 88
Day 62 (Joy back)	Day 79	Day 151
Day 76	Day 149	Day 43
Day 103	Day 198	Day 240
Day 144 (Joy back)	Day 266	Day 296
Day 154	Day 288	Day 102
Grace	**Trust**	**Clarity/ Uncertainty**
Day 84	Day 31	Day 22
Day 121	Day 182	Day 98
Day 142	Day 201	Day 117
Day 282	Day 240	Day 273
Day 38	Day 314	Day 339

Struggling	Purpose/Passion	Faith
Day 2	Day 10	Day 7
Day 51	Day 61	Day 14
Day 129	Day 107	Day 52
Day 139	Day 173	Day 106
Day 196	Day 210	Day 178
Day 206	Day 248	Day 192
Day 247	Day 306	Day 267
Day 308	Day 363	Day 313
Friends/Family	**Relationships**	**Alone**
Day 26	Day 32	Day 46
Day 75	Day 171	Day 105
Day 174	Day 226	Day 216
Day 268	Day 286	Day 271
Day 321	Day 341	Day 303
Forgiveness	**Anxious/Anxiety**	**Injury/Illness**
Day 77	Day 24	Day 28
Day 136	Day 87	Day 133
Day 195	Day 140	Day 193
Day 252	Day 239	
Day 322		

Peace	Pressure/Full Plate	Waiting
Day 13	Day 38	Day 9
Day 111	Day 97	Day 80
Day 161	Day 175	Day 122
Day 187	Day 199	Day 181
Day 222	Day 253	Day 191
Day 291	Day 262	Day 263
Day 352	Day 324	Day 316
Starting Over/ New Beginnings	**Tired/Rest**	**Overwhelmed**
Day 12	Day 49	Day 4
Day 48	Day 78	Day 36
Day 74	Day 86	Day 59
Day 110	Day 119	Day 91
Day 166	Day 159	Day 124
Day 184	Day 186	Day 145
Day 223	Day 208	Day 197
Day 227	Day 242	Day 245
Day 327	Day 311	Day 275
Day 344	Day 353	Day 351

Guidance/ Direction	Seeking Answers
Day 56	Day 9
Day 116	Day 40
Day 155	Day 127
Day 180	Day 146
Day 200	Day 207
Day 249	Day 235
Day 298	Day 274
Day 336	Day 317
Day 364	Day 360

Made in the USA
Monee, IL
10 May 2025